THE FORCE MULTIPLIER

How to Lead Teams
Where Everyone Wins

CONTENTS

INTRODUCTION

If you are dealing with the daily challenges of leadership or the stress and frustration of working for a bad boss, I know you don't have the time or energy to sift through loads of data to find something useful to help fix your problem. Although *The Force Multiplier* references research and hard data, it is written to be entertaining, practical, and simple to read. As a friend once told me, "When people deal with complex issues throughout their day, they want their people solutions to be simple." I couldn't agree more.

Because of that, this book is all about simple, real-world solutions that you can start (or stop) doing immediately in order to have a positive impact on how you work with others (and how others work with you).

This book contains many stories that are good and bad composites of bosses and their effects on people. There are benefits to using composites instead of detailing specific interactions:

1. *It allows you to realize that what you are encountering is not out of the ordinary.* It's easy to think you are in a unique or unusually bad situation. Although at times that is true, experience shows that much of what people go through is commonplace at work…it's happening to

everyone. Knowing this can help you avoid taking on an unnecessary amount of guilt or blame.

2. *These composites help keep fellow co-workers and bosses from feeling like they're being picked on or "called out" as bad examples.* All of these stories represent real people, but the names and sometimes the genders have been changed to protect the guilty.

Chapter 1

DO WE REALLY NEED ANOTHER BOOK ON LEADERSHIP?

Recently I strolled around a large bookstore and decided to go to the business section to see which leadership book was the "latest and greatest." It was overwhelming. I didn't know where to start. Nowadays, leadership (along with management) is a section and an industry unto itself. The topic has been addressed by a plethora of "expert" perspectives. Consulting firms have built entire business models on addressing the subject of leadership, while CEOs and other executives have achieved rock star status sharing their "secrets" to becoming a successful leader.

Now, don't get me wrong. I'm in no way bashing these books, authors, or celebrities. There is an absolute need for the books that have been written. With an increase in layoffs, downsizing, rightsizing, RIFs, and whatever other buzzword is or will be used to explain the need to reduce the number of workers, people are being asked (told) to do work that used to be done by two or three people...often with less training and fewer resources than were available before. Now more than ever, we need a better perspective on how to successfully lead people.

However, it wasn't the number of books in and of itself that was amazing to me. What I found curious was, given the number of books available about leadership, why were so many people still complaining about their bosses? You would think that these books would have improved the overall quality of leadership in the workforce, from entry-level managers to C-suite executives. Yet, it appears that this is far from the truth, and it's incredibly obvious. If you really question whether the overall quality of leadership in the workplace is decreasing, try this little experiment.

First, ask yourself: "How many bosses have I had in my life (parents and family members excluded unless you were employed by them)? Then ask: "How many good bosses did I have?" (Seriously. *Good* bosses...not mediocre, not acceptable, but good.) Then ask friends and colleagues: "Have you ever had three good bosses in a row? Or, how about two?" For most, the results are eye-opening. I have rarely had people tell me they had two good bosses in a row, and I don't recall anyone ever saying they had three.

As I travel around the world helping organizations solve their "people problems," I am constantly bombarded with stories about horrible interactions with bosses and executives. Lately, the stories seem to be getting worse. I'm not talking specifically about brand new managers who haven't figured out what they're doing yet. Most people understand that new managers need time to figure the whole "supervisor thing" out, and so they get a pass. The problem is you have people who have been managers, supervisors, directors, and even executives for a long time who are not only *ineffective* as leaders, but are actually the *reason* things aren't getting done. They're killing morale, quenching engagement, and destroying productivity. In fact, it seems that no matter where I am…at the gym, the airport, the coffee shop, or wherever I get into a conversation with someone and they ask what I do…the horror stories begin. It's as if there has never been a book written on the topic.

How could this be? My first thought was *maybe no one buys these leadership books.* Based on the number of these books on the "New York Times Bestseller" list, that's just not possible. Not only that, as I thought about the many meetings I've had with business leaders, managers, executives, and hiring professionals, most have a collection of the more prominent leadership and management books available on their bookcases right behind them.

Then I thought, *maybe people buy the books, but they just don't read them.* Now it is true that many people buy books and, at most, skim them. Many buy books and never crack open the covers. Some enjoy having the "hottest books" on their bookcases simply because it improves their image and gives them credibility as a leader. Many buy books with the best of intentions, but they never get around to reading them because life gets crazy. To be honest, I have a few books on my own bookcase that I have yet to read. But when it comes to reading resources on the topic of leadership, I don't believe that people just aren't reading them. I don't believe that this is the real problem.

The real problem became evident as I started skimming through some of these books. Many of these books talked about topics like: creating vision, changing culture, blazing new trails, and thinking big picture. Those are really good topics, but what about things like: "stop being a jerk" or "stop talking down to everyone and treating them like they are children" or "stop lying to people?" I noticed there was an absolute famine of books like that, and three problems became obvious:

1. *Most leadership books are written for high-level management positions.* They are written for people who are trying to change the culture of a department or company, people who are trying to instill a new mission or set of values within a large group of individuals, and people who are trying to "turn the ship." That's a great market, and there is certainly a need to increase both the quality and integrity of leadership at the top. We absolutely need to develop better executive-level leadership.

   But the reality is, the majority of people in leadership positions aren't CEOs. They're not executives. In fact, the majority of leaders are supervisors, team leaders, and managers—those on the front line. It's often the front-line leadership positions that determine whether a company succeeds or fails. They implement the vision given by top leadership, and they execute the decisions of the C-suite. They are the "make or break" level of the company. Not only do they have direct contact with non-managing associates, they also are often the ones having a direct impact on clients because they deal with the day-to-day running of the company.

My experience with these front-line leaders reminds me that they don't have the authority or position to do many of the things often associated with leadership—things like establishing a new mission or "turning the ship." Often, they're really as much followers as they are leaders. They don't get to set policies or determine the organization's vision—those things are handed down to them. They don't get to determine how the organization is going to change to adapt to future needs—that responsibility falls on the C-Suite. Front-line leaders get others to buy into the changes established by the leaders above them. Even for many at the executive level, they also have to be as much follower as leader because they have people to whom they report who set the directions for the company. The truth is, unless a person is at or near the top of the organizational food chain, there really are very few decisions they get to make.

2. *For most managers, setting policies, determining vision, and "turning the ship" are beyond their power and authority, as well as beyond the scope of their daily concerns.* As I've met and trained thousands of managers and supervisors across the country, I've seen that most couldn't care less about "turning the ship." They don't have the luxury of meditating on such thoughts. Their days are filled with meeting demands and putting out fires. The thought of how to turn the ship is quickly snuffed out by the questions of how to deal with someone who doesn't pull their weight, or how to train someone

who doesn't know how to do their job, or how to counter someone who has a bad attitude. They're trying to equip people to do their jobs while trying to keep them from knocking each other out! It's hard to think of C-level problems when you're dealing with a person whose mantra is "that ain't in my job description."

What these supervisors need is help with how to deal with the day-to-day people issues, not theories on how big corporations run. And the harsh reality is that if they don't learn how to manage these people issues, their chance of ever having the opportunity to be in position to actually turn the ship is minimal. If they do reach the executive level, they'll be ill-equipped to succeed because of huge leadership deficiencies. Even worse, if front-line leaders aren't properly equipped with the right skill sets to actually *lead,* the vision will never be reached, and the ship will never turn.

3. **Finally, most books focus only on what to start doing and not what to stop doing.** These books assume that, if a leader just adds a group of techniques or positive behaviors, everything else will fix itself. The truth is that, for many people in leadership positions, there are things they are already doing that limit their overall success.

Now, I'm not suggesting that managers don't need new skills and techniques to become effective leaders. Individuals must grow in organizational management, effective communication, assertiveness, delegation, performance management, and a litany of necessary leadership skills. In fact, some of these topics will be covered in this book. But I am convinced that, for a majority of people, there are also behaviors and habits that are *completely destroying* their ability to effectively lead others and *must be eliminated*. For some, it is being rude and insensitive. For others, it's being self-absorbed and narcissistic. For many, it is a fear or unwillingness to deal with conflict. While for others, it is being nitpicky or a perfectionist. The reality is you can have all the vision in the world, but if you come across as rude or a jerk, you're not going to consistently get the best out of people.

The challenge with these weaknesses is that, although some are aware of the presence of these weaknesses and are actively working to eliminate them, there are far more who either are completely unaware of their existence or, despite awareness, don't feel they are a barrier to effectiveness or feel any need to change. They feel that as long as they do a few basic things, they'll be fine ignoring their leadership shortcomings.

It's like having a professional basketball player who only focuses on offensive skills. They work on improving their scoring from every area of the court. They improve their post play. They perfect their mid-range jumper. They drive baseline repeatedly until it's impossible to stop them. They even work on their long-range shot so that they are finally a threat from the three-point area. The problem is they can't play defense. When they're on the court, it's like playing 4 on 5 because they are completely useless. They don't practice defense because they believe that, as long as they score points, they are helping the team. In fact, as long as they score enough points, they not only won't work on their defensive skills, they will quickly justify their lack of defensive prowess and attack anyone who criticizes them for it. The only time they are defensive is when you ask them about their defense.

Many "leaders" are the same way—ignoring their areas of weakness while working only on their strengths. They fail to realize their leadership is the sum total of the effect they have on those they lead. And although they may do a number of positive things, that positive effect is often negated by the bad things they do.

It's important to note that I'm not talking about people working primarily in their strengths. People like Marcus Buckingham, Tom Rath, and Jim Clifton have brought the idea of working in your strengths to the forefront, and I wholeheartedly agree with them. In fact, in many ways, the theme of this book correlates to the principle of working in your strengths while allowing others whose strengths differ from yours to work in theirs.

But this is not about just working in your strengths. This is about ignoring major flaws that affect your ability to positively influence others. Expecting to get great results while ignoring your own obvious flaws is like going to the doctor to lose weight and having her put you on an exercise program without saying you need to stop eating Twinkies. Just as it's unhealthy to assume that a patient doesn't need to stop bad eating habits, it's dangerous to assume that leaders don't need to stop doing bad leadership habits.

So, back to the original question: "Do we really need another book on leadership?" Yes, we do. The problem still exists. And as long as it exists, we'll need to keep addressing the issue in as many ways and from as many angles as possible…but in a *different* way. It needs to address the real core issues around why there is a lack of good leadership—not theoretical or big picture issues, but the issues that front-line managers face every day. Managers need a book that addresses the real consequences of poor leadership. It can't be just hype, it must be practical in a way that few books have been before.

This is that book.

Chapter 2

IS IT TRUE THAT THERE ARE NO GOOD PEOPLE OUT THERE?

Recently, I met with a group of friends for lunch for a purely social event. I hadn't seen most of them in quite a while, so we had a lot of catching up to do. We talked about all of the usual things…life, family, health, etc. As the night progressed and we began running out of things to say, I casually asked one of the gentlemen sitting across from me, who happens to be an HR Director, "How is work going?" I expected the cursory "fine." Boy, was I mistaken. He went on a rant. "It's so hard to find good people. People don't want to work nowadays. It's ridiculous the number of complainers we have." For the record, this is the standard rant I get from HR professionals, and the complaints were right on script.

After he finished complaining about how lazy people are and how it's hard to find good people, I casually mentioned that: "in general, employee engagement is a function of how employees are treated by their direct supervisors." And then, as though he were speaking as my surrogate, he just continued my thought, saying, "Yeah, many studies show that an employee's supervisor has the greatest effect on how engaged they are." He then cited the results of three surveys that reinforced his claim (actually my claim) as I sat there amazed. It was clear that we shared the same knowledge, but in the midst of the overwhelming reality of the problems he was facing, he reverted to blaming the employees. As Les Brown, the motivational speaker, used to tell me, "You can't see the picture when you're in the frame."

I've had this conversation more times than I can count. I think that I actually know this speech better than the flight attendant announcement about floatation devices and oxygen masks. I can't always tell you how it starts, but at some point, a manager says, "We need to figure out a way to hire better people. It's hard to find good people who work hard and show initiative. If we just hire the right people, we can increase our engagement." They'll often throw in, "This generation just doesn't like to work." It's as though there is something wrong in the hiring process and, if they can find a cure for it, all of their employee engagement problems will go away.

So, why is this happening? Executive coach Marshall Goldsmith describes many successful people as superstitious. Not superstitious in terms of not letting a black cat cross their path or not walking under a ladder. He describes successful people's superstition in terms of confusing *correlation* with *causality*.

Let's say a person does something...we'll call it X. If something good happens after doing X, it's easy and natural for the person to repeat the action (X) with the expectation that repeating X will bring results similar to the previous time. This is referred to as the Law of Effect. What is also natural for most people (especially successful people) is to attribute their success to X. Instead of recognizing that the successful result and what was done were two separate events that occurred together, many will conclude that the success was because of X.

It's possible that X was the source of their success. But it's also possible that doing X didn't contribute to their success at all. I remember a specific incident with a manager who was frustrated over how a project was progressing. Like most projects, it was over-budget, behind schedule, and no one wanted to take ownership of the problem. The manager, Sally, had a great reputation of being her associates' advocate. She always stood up for them, made sure they felt needed, and in general was just a nice person to work for. Also, in general, her direct reports worked hard for her.

But in this particular instance, things weren't going well, and she was feeling the pressure. Everything she did to try to get things back on track failed. Every approach, every technique, and every strategy just fell short. Finally, one day she let the pressure get the best of her and, in the middle of one of the meetings, she just exploded. She went on a tantrum, taking her frustration out on everyone in the room.

Afterward, Sally felt horrible and planned to pull her group together to apologize. But, before she could do that, an interesting thing happened—the project mysteriously got back on track. It was still over-budget, but it was no longer behind schedule, and people seemed to be working even harder to make sure it would be a success. Sally said to herself: "That's it! I found it! I finally figured out what works!

Yelling, screaming, and putting people down is what really makes people get work done. It's the secret to motivating people." Sally decided, at that moment, that being nice and friendly were weaknesses. They got in the way. She now knew what had to be done in order to be successful.

The problem is that Sally interpreted this as the basis for her success. However, her direct reports had a different perspective as to why things changed on the project. Although it is true they attributed the project getting back on track to that meeting, many of them reported that it wasn't Sally's berating of them that made them willing to work the long, extra hours to get things on track. To them, because acting that way was so out of character for Sally, they interpreted her tantrum as an indicator of just how overwhelmed she really was. They appreciated Sally and how she treated them, and they wanted to do everything in their power to make sure that she was successful and never experienced what she had felt again.

Unfortunately, Sally misinterpreted the cause of her success and believed that she'd discovered the key to leadership. All of the goodwill she had previously earned was slowly being poured down the drain. Over time, her team became less engaged. They still got things done, but they never performed the way they used to. They also were no longer as loyal to Sally as they previously had been. Some left the company for other opportunities. Others just checked out. Others didn't quit...not because of loyalty, but because they couldn't pull it off financially. But, they weren't there anymore either. They were AWP: Absent While Present. Sally found that she had to throw her occasional tirades to get people "off their butts and back to work" more frequently. But the more tantrums she threw, the less they worked.

Many successful leaders have crossed the same path as Sally. Whether it was tirades, micromanaging, or manipulation, they have done something that in the short term worked, but wasn't a real fix. They lucked out. They experienced a short-term success, but eventually the strategy was revealed to be defective. It didn't work consistently. It wasn't repeatable. It wasn't reliable. But that didn't stop them from using it.

Once these leaders determine that their strategy is successful, confirmation bias kicks in. Confirmation bias is when people look for information that confirms the pre-existing belief and ignores information to the contrary.

Here's how it works: Have you ever decided you needed to buy a car (new or used, but new to you)? Let's say you settled on a Pontiac Grand Am (I know that Pontiac is out of business, but no car company has offered me an endorsement deal so we're going with Pontiac). Once you decide on the car, it's amazing how many of those cars you begin to notice on the street. You see them wherever you go. The reality is they were there all along, you just didn't notice or recognize them. You literally didn't see them. Now that you're interested in them, they become a focus which makes you more aware of them.

Confirmation bias works the same way. You immediately notice the things that confirm what you already believe (what you want to see). The things that are contrary to what you believe are still there, but because you're not looking for them, you don't see them. Deep down, we all want to be right. More importantly, we don't want to be wrong. It's much easier to look at a situation and find reasons for you to be right vs. discovering reasons to have to change what you believe to be right. So, the brain makes it easy for us. We often only see or recognize the things that confirm what we already know.

So, for many managers, when what they're doing stops working, they don't come to the conclusion that their methods are wrong and they need to find a new strategy. It's much easier to just blame the people being managed. "If they were good people, they would respond to my awesome leadership skills. If the people aren't responding, it must be them. I need to go find some good people."

To make matters worse, these "successful" leaders, now convinced they were successful because of these flawed tactics, develop a leadership style that encapsulates all of the strategies they believe to work, even the bad ones. It's now their template for success. As their authority increases, they begin to implement new rules based on these behaviors. They create a culture that fosters these behaviors without ever measuring their effectiveness. They train new leaders to behave in this fashion. They coach and mentor ambitious future leaders using this template. They teach their template to other leaders and speak at conferences about the power of their template. This template becomes part of the leader's mantra, yet it only has a limited effect. But, they rarely go back and evaluate the template they've implemented to see if it was effective. It is now a "proven strategy" and part of their leadership dogma. It's infallible. Any failure cannot possibly be the fault of the template. It must be the people.

But was it ever really the people? I have a theory. I believe that most people actually want to do a good job at work. I know that this runs counter to the belief of many seasoned hiring professionals, but I still believe it. I believe that most people want to feel good about what they contribute on a daily basis, and work is a big part of that. In fact, I believe too many people tie their self-esteem not only to their titles at work, but also how their performance is perceived. Maybe that's true for you as well.

This is part of the reason people take a bad performance evaluation so personally. It's not just about the money— although money is important—it's about who we *are*. Doing a good job helps us feel good about ourselves.

I also believe that when people interview for a job, they don't just put their best foot forward to make a good impression. Okay, they do put their best foot forward to make a good impression, but I don't believe that who they are in the interview is significantly different than who they are at work. They sincerely plan on doing a good job. I just think that after people start working, something happens that derails all those good intentions.

Chapter 3

WHY I HATE MY JOB

Fran is very personable and charismatic, but above all she is smart...really smart. Fran sailed through high school and wound up at a top-tier university. After graduation, Fran worked for a few years, then she discovered her niche. It all seemed to happen as if by chance (or fate). She was given her first project to oversee because all the other Project Managers (the usual suspects) were focused on other, more important initiatives. The project was behind schedule and over budget. Fran began managing the project and took to it like the proverbial fish to water. Although Fran loved the business end of her job, she soon realized she had a gift and a passion for project management. Within a few months, she became the go-to person for important projects. Over time, the assignments grew from small projects to major initiatives. No matter what was given to her, she was always up to the challenge. Her career was fast-tracked. Fran was recognized by the top leaders as a superstar. She was given the nickname "the golden child."

Fran never pictured herself as a job hopper. In fact, in many ways she was just the opposite—she was extremely loyal, often to a fault. She didn't view moving from company to company as a legitimate way to advance a career. Fran endured corporate restructuring, RIFs (Reductions In Force), times of being under-staffed, and periods of economic instability, but remained faithful to her company. She had been approached by multiple headhunters over the years, each offering jobs with more responsibility and better pay, but she never truly entertained any of the offers. Even with its many shortcomings, she liked where she worked. She could see herself there long-term, plus the company's location made her commute reasonable. And, in spite of the occasional crazy person (because every company has at least one; if you don't know who the crazy person is in your office, it's because it's you), she liked her coworkers, too.

Then one day it finally happened—Fran was offered a huge promotion into her dream position. For years, she had worked her way up the ladder, constantly having to prove herself while honing her skills. She had built a great reputation and won the trust of many within her company, while turning down other more lucrative opportunities. It was finally all going to pay off. This would be her big chance; it was a golden opportunity. It was a chance to make her mark within the organization while utilizing the skills and experiences she had been gaining for the past 15 years.

There was only one problem: Steve. Steve's reputation within the organization was atrocious. He had a reputation of being difficult to work with. He was short-tempered, territorial, and constantly micromanaged everyone around him. Despite this and the fact that most in the organization knew this about Steve, he still managed to obtain a senior position.

Although Fran had never directly reported to Steve, she had worked with him on a number of major initiatives within the organization. Those times working with Steve confirmed everything she had heard about him. And he was the one thing standing between her and her dream job. Fran knew that having her dream job would also mean that Steve would be her boss. This caused her great apprehension.

At the advice of one of her mentors, Fran decided to meet with Steve before deciding on the position and express her concerns. During the meeting, Steve confided in her that he had been under tremendous stress due to a family situation as well as the pressure of recent layoffs and that what she had experienced was not who he really was. Steve assured her that he had no need or desire to micromanage her; she would have the freedom she needed to be effective. He told her, "I completely trust you which is why I specifically requested you for this position. It would make no sense for me to not let you do what I'm bringing you here to do in the first place." After doing a lot of soul searching, Fran decided this was an opportunity she just couldn't pass up and the risk was worth the reward. Worst case, she could ride it out a couple of years and then either move on to another position in the company or to another organization altogether. But, either way, this would be both a great experience and something that would look great on her resume. So, she went for it.

It only took a couple of weeks for Fran to realize she made a big mistake. Regardless of his promises, Steve was exactly who he had always been. He was not only nitpicking and micromanaging everything she did, he also began demeaning her in front of her staff. "Maybe he will change," she thought. "Maybe this won't be so bad once I'm used to it," she believed. She even rationalized the infamous, "I'm building character." But, soon she realized it just wasn't worth it. She began her search and, although the job market wasn't great, within a few months she had left the company for another job.

Let's think about this for a moment. Although Fran worked for a company that she respected, enjoyed her work, liked her coworkers, was well-compensated, and even worked within a reasonable commute from her house, she eventually left the company. And she didn't leave because she was offered a better position, she left because she was unhappy with her boss. That's incredibly important. Often things like compensation, interesting work, work-life balance, and upward mobility are cited by surveys as the things employees and employment candidates view as most important in a job. I do believe that each of those elements is essential to attracting good people, but experience and data tell me that, although those features may help attract talent, they rarely are enough to compensate for the presence of a bad boss. As Marcus Buckingham and Curt Coffman in their best-selling book, *First, Break All the Rules: What the World's Greatest Managers Do Differently* (Simon & Shuster, 1999), famously state, **"people leave managers, not companies."**

And Fran is in no way an anomaly. I spend most of my time working with organizations trying to improve their work environment in some form or fashion. The majority of the time, a problem had been brewing for a while, and it finally grew to the point where it could no longer be ignored or tolerated. And the only problems I deal with in the workplace are people problems (relationship issues). Whether they are looking for training, coaching, or consulting, these companies have finally come to the conclusion that their organization's people problems are hurting them enough that it's worth paying to address them. And let me tell you, Fran is in no way the exception to the rule. In fact, I have met hundreds of Frans. They may have had different faces and different locations, but all had one thing in common: regardless of all the other great benefits of working for their company, as well as how much they enjoyed their actual work, they now hated coming to work every day because of a bad boss, and it showed in their performance, their engagement, and their attitude.

This idea is echoed by Jack Zenger and Joseph Folkman ("Motivating People, How Damaging Is a Bad Boss, Exactly?" *Harvard Business Review*, July 16, 2012). They determined that, after studying the effectiveness of 2,865 leaders in a large financial services company and validating this information through the similar results of numerous surveys by multiple organizations, the overall leadership effectiveness of a boss (based on a 360 review) directly impacts not only employee satisfaction, but engagement and commitment as well. These results are not unusual. Study after study have produced the same conclusion: the number one factor affecting workers' effectiveness is their direct supervisor.[1, 2, 3]

Leaders really are the trump card when it comes to an effective workforce. Companies need to really ask themselves how good of a job are they doing when selecting and preparing leaders? The answer to this question has a direct impact on the company's bottom line.

Shouldn't we already know this? Isn't part of a leader's job to positively impact the performance of those they are leading? Isn't that the reason we have supervisors and managers in the first place? To an extent, we already *do* know this. The problem is that, in the moment, we are often so overwhelmed by the symptoms of a dysfunctional workplace, we forget to address the real disease. When employee engagement is down, when turnover is high, or when employee satisfaction is low, most organizations don't first look at the quality of their supervisors as being the likely source of their problem. Instead, almost reflexively, they blame the employees themselves for not being committed enough or lacking a strong work ethic, in spite of the all of the evidence to the contrary.

People often speak about employee engagement as though it is some strange abstract concept that requires some hidden, esoteric knowledge to understand. Employees are described as being engaged, fully engaged, disengaged, partly engaged, etc. Then, many of the solutions begin with things like aligning people to the organization's mission and so on and so forth. By the time we're all done, trying to find a real, practical, and workable solution to all of this engagement stuff is like trying to locate the Yeti or the Loch Ness Monster.

All of this engagement analysis is way too complicated. Let's make this really simple. Employee engagement is a measure of how much someone really cares about his or her job. I don't mean care if they *have* a job, but actually care about how they *do* their job. It's really that simple. That's why the phrase "emotional commitment" is so often used in describing engagement; it's a measure of how much someone is emotionally attached to his or her job. Everything else— enthusiasm, ownership, time at work, going the extra-mile, and even performance—is simply a symptom or indicator of whether engagement exists. These symptoms are signs of life, but not life itself. At the core, the real issue is how much does this person really care about his or her job?

For some, the entirety of that answer is internal. There are employees who work hard regardless of what's going on around them. They take ownership for their work even when surrounded by those who don't. Whether it's due to a sense of responsibility or their own sense of character and ethics, they will come to work and engage themselves regardless of the circumstances around them and how they are treated. These employees often perform *in spite of*, not *because of*, their manager and their work environment. But they are the exception, not the rule.

For the vast majority, work environment has a significant effect on engagement. Their manager, their coworkers, and their workplace culture play a substantial role in their ability to remain focused and engaged during the day. And in all honesty, in many cases, the work environment is sucking the life out of many employees and turning good employees into disengaged ones.

Employee engagement is a real problem. In 2016, Gallup determined that 32% of employees were engaged (up from 31.5% in 2014)[4]. That sounds like good news. Engagement is increasing, but let's not miss the reality: if 32% of employees are engaged, then 68% of employees are not engaged. Pause for a second and let that sink in—over 2/3 of American employees are not engaged. When you consider how that lack of engagement manifests into lost production, employee turnover, poor customer service, and missed opportunities, the costs are gargantuan. The only thing more alarming than all of this is that, for most, it's not alarming at all.

We've come to accept low engagement as the norm. Engagement statistics are provided by many reliable sources annually, and I've never read an article stating that these numbers should be cause for alarm. We would never accept these results in other areas of our lives. If you took your car to the mechanic and he (or she) said, "The problem with your car is that only 32% of your engine is working at full capacity," you wouldn't say, "Oh, well that doesn't sound too bad. How long can I drive it before it becomes a problem?" Assuming you have a mechanic who you trust, you would either pay the money to get the car functioning at an acceptable rate, like 100%, or you would decide that the car isn't worth the money and begin looking for another means of transportation.

If you went to the doctor for a checkup and she (or he) said, "Everything's fine except it seems your heart is only functioning at 32%," you wouldn't say, "Glad it's nothing serious." You would not only take whatever measures necessary to fix the issue, you would identify the root cause of the problem so that you would be assured that the problem never occurred again.

Unfortunately, we've come to accept and even expect mediocrity in the workplace. Engagement is a serious issue that needs to be addressed.

This can't all be blamed on "bad hires." Don't get me wrong—it is possible to hire the wrong employee. We've all made that mistake. Either they're not a good fit for the organization, they have their own agenda, or they look good on paper, but, in reality, are nothing like their resumes or represent a variety of other mistakes. But that still can't be the only problem. From personality assessments to all types of background checks, companies are doing everything possible to find the best possible candidate or at least weed out the potential bad hires. I'm far more concerned about the good people we hire who over time disengage. It's hard for me to imagine that companies are wrong about who they hire 68% of the time. There is something else going on, something that's happening *after* the hiring process.

The obvious place to look should be the managers. Organizations must be aware of what's going on with supervisors, managers, and other leaders. It's widely accepted that an employee's relationship with his or her direct manager or supervisor is the leading factor influencing employee engagement. So, if you really want to improve employee engagement, then address what's going on at the management level to give you the biggest bang for your buck. Jim Clifton, CEO of Gallup, is quoted as saying, "Here's something they'll probably never teach you in business school: The single biggest decision you make in your job—bigger than all of the rest—is who you name manager. When you name the wrong person as manager, nothing fixes that bad decision. Not compensation, not benefits—nothing."

What is really eye-opening is the state of the engagement level of the managers. An oft-neglected fact about the Gallup's research[5] is that, among job categories, managers, executives, and officers had the highest levels of engagement in 2014 at 38.4%. That means more than 60% of those in leadership positions were not engaged. These are the people who are coaching, training, and mentoring other managers. These are the one's creating your "culture." If *they're* not engaged, imagine what they're giving to their direct reports.

But this shouldn't be surprising either. Managers are still employees, and most still have others to report to. Do you really expect the student to surpass the teacher?

Of course, there are other questions that need to be asked, as well: How is the overall work environment? Does the company really value its employees? Are people's daily responsibilities aligned with their skillsets? Do people really know how to perform their work? And yes, are you hiring the right people? But let's start with the managers and supervisors.

For executives and business owners, this should be an eye opener. These are the people who are often focused on trying to address low engagement and high turnover in their organization. Instead of trying new recruiting methods to weed out the uncommitted and avoid the job hoppers, it's time to start focusing on what to do with people once they become employees. Who's managing them? In fact, are there pockets of high turnover within your organization? Look at the manager. How is he doing? Is she the right person for the job? Did we really do a good job in selecting them and setting them up for success? What have we done to equip them and prepare them to lead and engage people? Would any sane, non-masochistic person work for them?

You can hire and train good leaders to create a culture that fosters engagement, and then hire good people to foster that culture, or you can ignore the problem and let your culture contaminate the good people you hire.

But there's one question we haven't asked yet: What is a good leader?

Chapter 4

FORCE MULTIPLIER

Last year, I hosted a party for one of my closest friends. This guy is special. He's one of those people who lights up a room when he walks in. He seems to connect with everyone around him regardless of their similarities or differences. He has this uncanny ability to gauge the temperature of the room and know when to be fun and when to be serious. This is "my guy!" And it's not just the two of us. Our wives have become extremely close. His young children view my two teenage boys as older brothers. Our families are intertwined.

That made it all the more difficult when we found out that he would be deployed to Afghanistan where he would spend the next year aiding the military reduction in force. Because of our relationship, we decided to host a going away party for him. It was a small gathering of thirty or so of his closest relationships.

We ate, we laughed, we cried. As he sat in my living room pondering his uncertain future, we circled around him and his family. We then each took turns expressing our love for him and his family, providing words of encouragement, and vowing to protect and help provide for his wife and their two young children in whatever way necessary while he was gone.

As we went around the room, there was one person whose words I personally had been waiting to hear—a high-ranking officer in the army. He was a career officer who had seen a number of those under his command being relocated, as well as having been relocated himself many times. Over the course of his career, this officer had attended many of these "deployment parties," as he called them, and he was also a mutual friend of ours. I knew his perspective would be unique. But I was in no way prepared for the lasting effects his words would have on my perspective of leadership.

The officer began by saying, "You are what we in the army refer to as a '**force multiplier**.' The overall effectiveness and output of your group is increased by your very presence. Because of your personality and character, you bring out the best in each and every resource you come into contact with, and you increase the value of all of our assets."

A force multiplier is a machine which allows large loads to be moved by a small effort. Some examples of force multipliers include: gear, wheelbarrow, pulley, and lever. The military adopted the term to describe something that increases the combat value of other assets. It's usually used in reference to some type of tool, strategy, or technology that makes other things like weapons, hardware, or troops more effective in combat. For example, a shovel is also a force multiplier because it enables a person to dig faster and more effectively than they could with their bare hands. A machine gun is also a force multiplier. Force multipliers usually refer to things, although the definitions can be expanded to include people and characteristics.

As obvious as this should have seemed, it's as if my eyes were opened for the very first time and a whole new world opened up for me. For years, the idea of being a supervisor or manager was almost synonymous with doing nothing. It had become a running joke. I can think of times when I've helped a friend move (which honestly has been too many times), and one person was caught doing nothing while the rest of us were working. Once called out, their immediate response would be, "Oh, I'm supervising."

As a person who trains leaders, I often hear experts and even other leaders give all types of definitions of what a leader is. I've heard that leaders have followers, and I believe that's true. I've heard that leaders get people to work together to accomplish a common goal, and I certainly can't argue with that. I've heard others say that leadership is all about being a servant or about humility or about the ability to get people to do things they wouldn't do on their own. But, whether referring to the ability to provide vision and direction, the ability to solve problems, or the ability to motivate others, there is one question that is rarely asked when talking about leadership effectiveness: *"Is more accomplished by the person's presence than what would have occurred if they weren't there?"*

This is the question that is never asked. Even if it were, most in a leadership position wouldn't be able to answer it honestly and accurately. Most, if asked this question regarding themselves, would immediately respond "of course." But think about it for a minute. Do most leaders really multiply output? Do they really leverage and maximize the strengths of the individuals they lead? That takes a lot of work and energy, not to mention the mental work of discovering the motivating forces of the individuals under your charge.

That's the whole point of understanding different personalities. A few fortunate souls seem to have found this holy grail of leadership. Somehow, they have learned to do what others haven't—get the best out of everyone they lead, not just a few. This attribute shouldn't be reserved for the only the most privileged leaders. We heap praise on hall of fame coaches and applaud leaders of movements for being able to get the best out of people. Shouldn't this be the norm? Shouldn't this at least be one of the criteria for being called a leader in the first place?

In all honesty, a lot of "leaders" don't really lead. They're far from being force multipliers. Many have a complete misunderstanding of what leadership is. They tell and direct, but they don't engage the disengaged. Others lack the skill or vision that it takes to motivate, inspire, and leverage the strengths of a group. They are only capable of directing people and teams who are already engaged. It's one thing to steer a rocket in the right direction; it's a whole different thing to get that rocket off the ground.

I remember a conversation with a friend who was looking for a new job. I asked him what things he was good at, and the first thing he said was "managing people." I asked him if that was really one of his skills (that should have been a hint). His response was yes, as long as I have people who want to work. His view of leadership had nothing to do with being a catalyst for results, it was more a function of giving direction to people who were already focused, motivated, and productive. He wasn't thinking like a force multiplier; he was thinking like a force director.

Being a force multiplier is not the only characteristic of a leader. I don't even think it should be used as the sole definition of a leader. There are a lot of other very important attributes needed in leadership. But, in all honesty, without leaders being force multipliers, how necessary are they?

In fact, due to the lack of force multipliers in leadership positions, many companies have begun questioning the necessity for supervisors. Recently, I heard an interview with the owner of an international start-up company. As he discussed his business model, he casually mentioned that he has no real managers. There is a top-level leadership team, but below that he doesn't hire people to manage his staff. His reasoning was that they weren't necessary. He decided that, if he hired the right people, he didn't need managers. And, based on the previously used definitions of a leader, I'm inclined to agree with him.

There really isn't a need for mediocre or ineffective leaders, especially if you hire properly motivated people. But if this business owner had experienced even one force multiplier, his perspective would have been different. He never would have decided that he didn't need someone who makes his employees better and increases their effectiveness. That would always be beneficial not only to the company, but to the workers as well. A force multiplier is never expendable.

Chapter 5

THE RELATIONSHIP BANK

Years ago, I was introduced to a concept that, on the outside, seemed both simple and obvious, yet it was a complete paradigm shift for me. It's been instrumental in allowing me to build and maintain great relationships, and it will help you as well. It's unique in that it applies to most any type of relationship you can think of. Whether friendships, business associates, customer service, or romantic relationships, it governs what will make the relationship work or what will cause it to fall apart. It functions like a natural law. The idea is that of a Relationship Bank.

To understand the concept of a relationship bank, think of everyone you know, including yourself, as having (or being) a bank. For you, every person you know has an account in your bank, thus every relationship you have is represented by an account in your relationship bank. What drives the bank are your interactions with others. Whether we're aware of it at the time or not, almost every interaction with someone is either a positive or a negative experience. Those interactions act as transactions in your bank. Positive interactions leave a positive emotional byproduct we'll call a deposit. Negative emotional experiences create a negative emotional byproduct we'll call a withdrawal.

Suppose you're a supervisor and get a new employee named Jan. You and Jan hit it off immediately. She's a great worker, and you view her as such. You decide to let her know how excited you are to have her on the team and that you're available if she has any questions or concerns. If that experience is viewed as positive by Jan, it becomes a deposit.

Notice, I said, "If that experience is viewed as positive by Jan, it becomes a deposit." That is really important. Deposits and withdrawals are completely subjective, and the one who determines whether it is a deposit or a withdrawal is the bank into which the transaction is made. That means that when it comes to transactions, it's not the *intent* that determines whether or not the interaction is positive or negative, it's the *impact*. During an interaction, impact is more important than intent.

Often people intend to have a positive interaction with others, but for various reasons it doesn't always turn out that way. There are times when a wife comes home and begins to complain to her spouse about some event that occurred earlier that day. Often, the spouse thinks the best way to make a deposit is to provide a solution to the perceived problem; yet, most times what the wife really wants is for the spouse to just listen to her. Even though the spouse intended to have a positive interaction, the impact was negative. Because of this, it must be remembered that the best gauge for determining whether or not an interaction is a deposit or a withdrawal is the bank, not the account holder. The bank determines whether or not the interaction was a deposit or a withdrawal.

Just like in a real bank, these deposits and withdrawals affect the overall balance of the account held at each bank. Your balance in a person's account determines how much they trust you, how loyal they'll be to you, and even how much they like or, in the case of intimate relationships, love you. This balances affects the lens through which you see people. It governs how people interpret not only other people's actions, but the perceived intent behind those actions.

As your balance increases, the relationship grows stronger. A person's view of you becomes more favorable. This increased emotional connection will translate into greater trust, empathy, and loyalty. If you are their manager, you will find people more receptive to your input and direction. People will be easier to lead. Even when giving corrective action, you will find that people are more receptive because they believe you have their best interests at heart. And, when you have a large balance, you are more likely to receive the benefit of the doubt when you mess up.

But, as your balance is reduced, the relationship becomes weak. You become emotionally disconnected. With this disconnect, trust is often damaged, and loyalty is diminished. As a manager, you'll find that it takes more work to get people to follow your direction and often, when they do, it's not a wholehearted effort. Low-balance managers have to rely on their authority and title to prod people into work. They continually have to push and push because they've sucked much of the internal motivation out of people. It's easy for low-balance managers to get frustrated with their direct reports' lack of engagement. Unfortunately, what they do when frustrated often leads to more withdrawals.

There is another advantage to having a high relationship bank account balance with people. When you have a high balance, it is actually easier for you to make additional deposits. Because of your strong connection, your actions are interpreted in a positive light. Not only in what you do, but your intent. Truly, the rich get richer. Conversely, if the account has too little of a balance or goes negative, it becomes even more difficult to rectify. Every action is interpreted through a lens of dislike and distrust. Even when considerable effort is made to make an investment in the relationship, there will be a period where even the positive actions are questioned. Instead of thoughts of thanks, you get, "I wonder what he or she wants?" This is the natural consequence of a damaged relationship.

This metaphor is a simple way of saying that your relationships are defined by the cumulative effect of the transactions you have with the people you interact with over time, not just the current interaction. And the balances of those accounts vary over time. But, don't let the simplicity of the metaphor fool you. It's very important. People often forget that our interactions don't happen in a vacuum. They're a function of our previous interactions.

All deposits and withdrawals aren't the same. The amount deposited or withdrawn varies in magnitude. Just as the bank determines whether or not it's a deposit, the bank also determines the value of the transaction, not the account holder.

If an interaction makes the person feel pretty good, it is a smaller deposit than an interaction that make them feel great. It's completely subjective.

There are some very specific factors that help determine value of the transaction.

One is the *level of impact.* The level of impact is a measure of the effect of the interaction as interpreted by the bank. For example, if someone forgets to do something and the result is a slight nuisance, then it will likely be a small withdrawal. But if the same act causes a public embarrassment or a lost opportunity for a promotion, it will likely be a much larger withdrawal.

Another is *the dimension of trust that was affected.* Things that appear to be intentional— positive or negative— will almost always have a greater impact and thus be worth more than things that seem accidental. Violations based on things like integrity, character, and agenda are almost always interpreted as more severe and damaging than violations that are a function of a person's inability. As you will see in later chapters, this area is also completely subjective and varies greatly from person to person.

Number of prior violations. When there is a clear pattern of prior trust violations, even if they are each relatively minor when viewed in isolation, the overall pattern may be deemed a serious breach. As the proverbial "straw that broke the camel's back," it is the pattern of trust violations that provides evidence that the offender is not worthy of future trust. However, when there are few past violations, any given trust violation may be viewed as the exception rather than the rule.

The one exception to this is that, at times, a large withdrawal from someone who's close or trusted can have a greater impact than the same coming from someone you're not as close to.

Here is a true story of the power of this concept. Years ago, I was scheduled to speak at a retreat. I wasn't just scheduled to speak at the retreat, I had organized and was hosting this weekend long retreat. A week before the retreat was scheduled to happen, a close friend's mother passed away.

I had an unfortunate decision to make. On one hand, I had a close friend mourning the loss of his mother, and on the other I had nearly 100 people who had paid to attend this retreat and arranged months in advance to attend. It was a no-win situation. In retrospect, I wish I had gone to the friend in advance and asked for his input. That would have been much smarter, but things are always easier to see after the fact. What I did was send flowers, a card, and a close friend to represent me, and I facilitated the retreat.

Of course, I felt guilty about this decision. It ate at me. A week or so later, I went to the friend's house. He talked about the service and how he was able to memorialize his mother in a way he felt properly represented her life. We laughed. We cried. I apologized for not attending the service. I shared that I wanted to be there and just didn't know what to do. This friend, who had been introduced to the same concept a few years prior, then looked at me and said, "It's Okay, Tony you have enough deposits with me. We're all good." It's hard to fully communicate the weight that was lifted off of my shoulders that day.

Although my friend is a very gracious person, you can't underestimate the contribution that our ongoing friendship played in his response. Even though this isn't a work-related example, you should know I've had similar experiences in the workplace more times than I can count.

What follows is a list of deposits you can make to keep your relationship bank account full with those you work with and care about. There is also a list of withdrawals that you should try to avoid. We'll explore how these deposits and withdrawals occur for the four personality styles in the upcoming chapters.

21 Common Deposits

1. **Being fair and consistent**
   Always treating everyone by the same standards and valuing them as human beings. Not playing favorites.

2. **Treating everyone with dignity and respect**
   Regarding each person's abilities, strengths, and/or achievements. This is shown by expressions of praise, admiration, and efforts made to seek their input or expertise.

3. **Involving others in decision making**
   Pulling in associates and letting them take part in the decision-making process. This also includes hearing their suggestions even if their suggestions don't influence the outcome.

4. Having a positive attitude

Having a consistent enthusiastic attitude. Not just a positive attitude that is based on the situation, but one that remains enthusiastic regardless of the circumstances.

5. Giving recognition for a job well done

Giving praise when people achieve something or go above and beyond what is expected or the call of duty.

6. Apologizing/Accepting responsibility for mistakes

Saying "I'm sorry" (actually saying those words or something of equal value) and taking full responsibility for errors, mistakes, and misjudgments, without adding "but" or explaining how it wasn't really your fault.

7. Remembering special events (birthdays, etc.) and life situations

Celebrating special events and expressing empathy by displaying the appropriate emotional response to current events affecting the lives of people.

8. Knowing the individual

Taking the time to know co-workers on an individual level. Not necessarily being "best buds," but getting to know them as a person.

9. Face-to-face communication

Using positive expressions, body language, and voice inflection to convey non-transactional messages where tone could be misinterpreted in written communication.

10. Honesty/Openness

Consistently expressing the facts even about difficult news and sharing your feelings about that news.

11. Assistance without judgment

Offering help with job responsibilities, interpersonal conflict, or decision-making without its having a negative impact on future decisions or the relationship as a whole.

12. Consistent communication/effective communication

Using the various communication vehicles available to convey information on a regular basis.

13. Flexibility

Allowing individuals the freedom to find their own unique ways to accomplish tasks and solve problems when appropriate.

14. Built trust

Identifying what makes people believe that you are reliable, honest, and willing to advocate for them and then taking steps consistently to exhibit those qualities in your interactions with everyone.

15. Loyalty

Having faithful allegiance and constant support.

16. Predictability/Consistency

Exhibiting the same behavior and responses to similar situations.

17. Clearly defined expectations

Stating verbally and in written form what you expect the organization, teams, and individuals to achieve. Expectations should be Specific, Measurable, Attainable, Realistic, and given a Timeframe (SMART).

18. Accurate information

Sharing data or communicating information that has been confirmed as being factual.

19. Dealing with tough situations

Showing emotional stability, integrity (honesty), and willingness to get others involved to address a difficult situation.

20. Transparency

Establishing a reputation for being consistently open and clear about the status of the organization or an issue.

21. Forgiveness

Showing that a mistake or offense will not be held against someone. This is done first by expressing forgiveness directly to the person and then by intentionally not bringing up the issue again to anyone.

20 Common Withdrawals

1. Not listening

Physically not paying attention when people are speaking; showing annoyance or indifference about what people are saying.

2. Failing to give recognition

Omitting praise when people achieve something; failing to plan celebrations for major accomplishments.

3. Stealing credit

Attributing success or achievement to one's self instead of acknowledging everyone who contributed; outright taking credit for what belongs to someone else.

4. Giving responsibility without authority/Not providing proper resources

Giving a duty or assignment to a person without making them accountable and without providing either the authority or means needed for success.

5. Playing favorites

Consciously or unconsciously showing preference for certain people. This behavior is demonstrated by the amount of time spent with certain people, opportunities that are granted only to certain people, and/or by recognition and praise that is only given to certain people.

6. Constant criticism and destructive comments

Tendency to make negative statements about people's performance or character. This is particularly harmful when done publicly or as a form of humor.

7. Bursts of anger/Fits of rage

Inability to control emotional responses during stressful situations or when angry; using profanity, yelling, pounding on furniture, and slamming doors are examples of bursts of anger.

8. **Gossip**
   Sharing details about private discussions or sensitive information about others without their permission.

9. **Lying/Dishonesty**
   Intentionally withholding or distorting some or all of the facts.

10. **Unresolved issues**
    Failing to address both performance and behavioral issues.

11. **Not owning mistakes**
    Making excuses or denying responsibility for a mistake.

12. **Too busy for others**
    Having the appearance of being unavailable, or stating one's lack of availability.

13. **Setting a bad example**
    Exhibiting behavior that is opposite what one has been proclaiming as the expected or standard behavior.

14. **Usurping authority**
    Showing disregard for established authority through open criticism or secretly doing things that go against the authority.

15. **Passive/Aggressive**

    Indirectly resisting to avoid conflict; examples include procrastination, sabotage, and phrasing an objection in a sarcastic or rhetorical manner. ˙

16. **Not giving enough information**

    Communicating inconsistently and without providing adequate details.

17. **Blaming/pointing fingers**

    Assigning and placing extreme emphasis or blame in situations where who's at fault is not clear. Focusing on who is to blame when it is a minor issue compared to the solution.

18. **Adding your two cents**

    Providing unsolicited opinion in a rude manner. Constantly trying to prove how smart you are.

19. **Unnecessary conflict/stress**

    Using conflict or stress as a management tool. Playing devil's advocate.

20. **Keeping people in the doghouse**

    Refusing to forgive a mistake; consistently reminding the offender and others of the mistake; refusing to give the offender a chance to do anything else for fear that they will make the same mistake.

Why am I doing all of this talking about relationships? What does this have to do with leadership? Everything! Whether you're leading a team, a project, or a change implementation, what you are really doing is leading people. Leadership is always about leading people; it's people who have to fulfill the mission. It's people who have to embrace a new situation and carry out the corresponding change. It's people who get things done. Leadership is always about leading people. And leading people is always about relationships.

What we are talking about is the ability to build an emotional connection with the people you work and interact with. Another word for this would be *emotional commitment*. Almost every organization that studies employee engagement will tell you that emotional commitment drives engagement. Emotional commitment is king.

People are driven to work harder, go the extra mile, and take ownership of their jobs when they are emotionally invested. Emotional commitment even trumps logical commitment. Most people will give more effort because they are emotionally invested than they will if they are only working because it is the right thing to do. And statistically, what relationship drives engagement more than any other? Drum roll please...a person's relationship with their direct supervisor.

For leaders, understanding relationship banks and account balances is the key to building loyalty, commitment, and engagement. The more committed a person is to his or her direct supervisor (as well as the company and coworkers), the more engaged he or she will be. And that leads to greater output and greater employee retention. Leaders who have great relationships with their people are far more effective— not only at being productive, but at retaining and developing talent. Relationships are everything to a leader. Without them, all you have is authority, and you'll find that, if that's all you rely on, you'll never be an effective leader.

The problem with many "leaders" is thinking that relationship-building is not valuable. For some reason or another, it's not a priority to them. Some think it's just a waste of time. Others don't want to be "all touchy feely."

Chapter 6

NO SILVER BULLET

Many books claim to contain the 1, 2, or 3 secrets of successful leadership. They sell the silver bullet: the hidden strategy that will turn you into a leader supreme. Everyone will follow you, and you will be able to effectively lead any team to the highest levels of productivity. There's a big problem with that idea. In the real world, there is no silver bullet!

Leading people is complex, far too complex to think that one thing or one rule will cover everybody. This is a thinking person's game. The search for an easy way will lead to great disappointment and frustration. As a friend used to say, "This ain't grits where you just add water and stir."

What makes leadership so complex is people. People don't come in one flavor—they have many differences that make people who they are. Whether it is the difference in gender, difference in cultures, difference in belief systems, or the different experiences that shape and mold how they think and what they value, these differences will have a great effect on what it takes to lead them effectively.

For example, in the last chapter, I included a list of common deposits and withdrawals. Although some, like *being fair and consistent*, are universal…others, like *predictability*, are a deposit only for certain individuals. These transactions vary based on the individual's needs, as well as that person's.

It's these differences that many leaders don't consider when leading their teams. People's distinctiveness is often the very thing that keeps leaders from being successful. Many have a leadership "style" they use. That style turns out to be effective to certain levels, but that effectiveness varies from person to person. There are people who end up being easy to lead. Working with them is almost natural. There are others who are far more difficult to lead. What works with others doesn't seem to work with them, and it's frustrating. But, often it's not that the person is difficult to lead—it's that they're difficult for *you* to lead *them*. If another leader with a completely different leadership style and philosophy stepped in, that previously "difficult" person may thrive under the new leadership.

Although there are some people who are truly difficult, are aware of it and do it intentionally, others are completely unaware they are being difficult. The reality is that many of the people we find difficult are just different, different from us. They have different emotional needs, different behaviors, and different motivators than we do. Not being aware of or understanding those differences is often the source of friction and frustration in the workplace. The overwhelming majority of conflict happens not because of malicious intent, but because of miscommunication and misunderstandings. And often the source of those misunderstanding is our differences.

What separates the great leader from the average leader is what I call *style flexibility*. Style flexibility is the ability to identify and adapt to the different needs, behaviors, and motivators of the various people you lead. It's a type of situational leadership that allows a leader to be effective with everyone they lead, not just the people who naturally respond to their approach. The average leader has his or her own style and expects everyone to conform to that style. Leaders with style flexibility modify their style and thus their strategies to get the best out of everyone. These leaders are far more likely to succeed with leading various types of people than the leader who sticks to one leadership style.

One of the most fundamental yet common differences people experience when working together is personality, and it is often a source of friction and conflict. Unlike gender or race, personality doesn't carry with it obvious visual indicators; thus, it's not always immediately obvious that there are differences when you meet someone. But personality differences are often there, and they can have a huge impact on people's ability to connect with one another and their ability to work together.

For example, take one of my clients, John. John is all about getting things done. He's a doer, and he does everything quickly. He thinks quickly, talks quickly, and decides quickly. This is the very thing that has led to his success. Everyone at the company knows that once you put John on an assignment, things are going to happen.

But John has a problem...Fred. John manages Fred. Fred is not like John. Fred is a planner, and he's all about the details. He's not a bottom-line type of guy. He is far more methodical than John. To Fred, accuracy is far more important than speed, so he always makes sure that John has all of those details. All of them! When John needs information from Fred, he's usually in a hurry and ready to make decisions, so he just wants the bottom line so he can move on. But that's not what Fred gives him. In fact, often Fred doesn't initially give him anything but more questions. And it bugs John to no end. John doesn't understand Fred. Often, all he wants is an update on a project, but John can't get Fred to give him what he wants the way he wants it, so John considers Frank difficult.

Fortunately, it is possible to not only manage these differences, but to leverage them. We've all had to experience personality issues, and they permeate almost every area of our lives. Our personality differences can either work for us or against us, and, by understanding the perspective of different personalities, we can connect with virtually anyone we interact with. Henry Ford once said, "If there is any secret to success, it lies in the ability to get the other person's point of view and see things from that person's angle as well as your own." Whether it is our relationship with coworkers, our romantic interest, or our own children, the ability to connect with and influence people who have personalities different than our own is vital to our success and happiness.

Unfortunately, doing this is anything but natural. We human beings have this tendency to look at ourselves in a way that is favorable. In fact, we often have an inflated perception of ourselves. Psychologists refer to this as self-enhancement. When it comes to positive things, we overestimate how likely we are to do something good, but are much more objective in our view of strangers.

Interestingly, when it comes to doing things that aren't so favorable, we cut ourselves some slack; we give ourselves more grace than we do strangers. It's different when it's you because you know the background of the situation. You know why you made the decision you did, and you know your intentions. If something goes awry, you can easily blame another person or the circumstances and give yourself a break. You're not a bad person; you just were placed in a bad situation.

Then there's this thing called *affinity bias*. Simply put, we are more comfortable with and tend to like people who we view as being like us. In fact, we actually use the same parts of our brain to think about ourselves as we use to think of those who are like us. This means we give those we view as being like us the same breaks we give ourselves. Thus, we're more likely to be patient and empathetic to people we view as being like us. Conversely, we're more likely to view people we see as different from us with indifference and even contempt.

This causes us to make ourselves the norm. We become the standard. Our strengths are normal, and our weaknesses are acceptable. When people are like us, they are normal, and anything or anyone that differs from us is often viewed negatively. The problem is, when it comes to personality, it's far more likely that people will be different from us than like us.

Even beyond this, because we view ourselves as the norm, we try to treat people the way we want to be treated. This is natural. Why wouldn't people want the same things we do? So, we show appreciation to people the same way we'd like to receive it. We give affection the same we want to receive it. And we lead others the way we want to be led or think we should be led. And when that doesn't work, we view them as difficult and our affinity for them plummets.

I know there are methods for looking at our differences that are far more complex than what we are going to address in this book. Some systems have more categories of people, others have more combinations. As I eventually began training leaders (I have literally given some form of personality assessment to thousands if not tens of thousands of leaders), I utilized a variety of different instruments to make leaders more effective. Some worked better than others. The more I worked with people, the less enamored I became with the sophistication and complexity of the instrument, and the more I became focused on the practicality and usability of the instrument.

Complexity is not necessarily a bad thing when looking at your own personality, but the goal is not to just focus on yourself. Although there is a fair amount of self-discovery and self-affirmation that occurs when looking at this, the goal is beyond just your view of yourself. The real power comes when you use the tools to enhance how you interact with your boss, coworkers, subordinates, spouse, kids, etc.

The problem is that the more complex the system, the harder it is to keep track of and even remember the results. I know people who have taken very popular assessments and can't even remember what category they fell into. If they can't remember that, how will they ever remember the categories of others and how to apply it to relationships? The more complex the instrument, the more difficult it is to keep track of all the different people with whom you're connecting.

Also, people's lives are already complex. Most either have work that is complex, or they're doing a job that used to be done by two or three people. Experience tells me that people like this would prefer to have simple solutions to their people problems.

In general, people fall into four different categories. Over the next four chapters, you will be introduced to these personality types. Each personality has been given a specific name. These names were chosen as they represent some significant aspect of the nature of that type. The names are not perfect, as I believe that due to people's individuality there is no perfect way to categorize people.

One thing you will notice about the names is that they all represent some positive aspect of the personality. This was done intentionally. Historically, certain personality types were valued in the workplace and especially in leadership roles more than others. This promoted somewhat of an unspoken hierarchal view of the types. In some of the systems, the very names used expose that hierarchal view. Those personalities that are viewed more favorably receive a more attractive name, like warrior, champ, etc. Others have names that are closer to being derogatory, like lamb or human computer.

The reality is, the workforce has changed from an industrial, labor-driven workplace to a technology, creativity, and service-driven workplace. With that has come the realization that organizations don't just need our workforce to reflect one type, but they need to have the positive attributes of each personality represented at every level of influence. This has been shown to be true regardless of whether it's a public or private sector, non-profit, or religious organization. Even the military has seen a shift in culture as diplomacy is needed more and more in this ever-changing global community we're a part of. A bias toward certain personalities and against others can unknowingly contribute to an organization's not realizing its full potential.

Two warnings: first, this system is not intended to make anyone an expert on people in any way. You should not think that all of a sudden you've become a psychotherapist after reading this book. You may laugh, but I present lots of programs, and it's easy to for people to think "I've got people all figured out" based on a few hours of exposure to a new topic.

Second, you need to be careful not to overuse or stereotype people because of these categories. This is a tool and only a tool. Because we humans are subjected to so much information on a daily basis, we tend to take information and put it into categories. It just makes life much easier to deal with. That is how our brains work.

The problem is that, with these categories, we make associations and apply them beyond what is true or has been verified. We also can make these certain characteristics universal and think that every person within a certain personality type must have this behavior in common. This is especially true if you've had bad experiences with them or they rubbed you the wrong way. When we do this, we create biases. The problem is that we are still uniquely individual. Although they may have similarities, all MCs, for example, or any other category aren't the same. This stereotyping is not just limited to personalities, but we'll save that for another book.

As you will see, personalities have strengths and weaknesses. One thing that determines whether a personality is working in their strengths or weaknesses is how much their personality's needs are being met. Often, when people are primarily displaying their weaknesses, there is a need not being met. Just as when a person is sick, they display some sort of symptom, the same is true of the personalities. Often what we see and what irritates us is not the actual disease, it is the symptom.

That should give us a bit of comfort. It is easy to take any of the personalities' difficult behavior personally. I remember one afternoon my wife and I were having a disagreement. It wasn't that we were in the middle of some battle, we just weren't connecting and we were starting to get on each other's nerves (I know you can't relate because that has never happened to you). I can't even remember what it was about, because honestly it wasn't that serious, but in the moment it seemed that everything she did just made me more and more irritated. It seemed as though she knew everything to say to get under my skin. As we stood in the kitchen, with me visibly upset, she made the most timely statement.

She said, "You know, I'm not trying to frustrate you." At that moment, it was like a fog lifted. Even though nothing changed, I needed to hear that. I was taking every part of our conversation and assuming an intent behind it. I needed to remember that we're on the same team. I needed to be made aware that this wasn't anything malicious, we just weren't connected.

In the same way, many times when people are exhibiting their negative behaviors, they are not doing it with the intention of frustrating those around them. Often, they're not even aware that their behavior is difficult. Knowing this can make it easier to deal with their behavior without taking it personally. Yeah, they're being a jerk, but they don't even know it so don't let it mess you up. It's so easy to get caught up emotionally by people's behavior that we begin responding based on our emotions rather than in a way that is constructive.

Which brings us to the part that is counterintuitive: The cure to getting the personality out of their weakness and into their strengths and to dealing with their difficulties, is to meet the unmet need. That sounds simple. Just meet their need. The problem is that in the moment, meeting their need is often the last thing you want to do. If a conductor is curt, defensive, and disrespectful, most people's natural inclination is not to give them control or show them respect. In fact, we often want to do the opposite because we feel they don't deserve respect or should be in control in that moment. Although this may make us feel better in the moment, it is actually counterproductive in that the need remains unmet; thus, the conductor is still behaving out of their weakness, which means they're still a pain to deal with.

One of the greatest pieces of relationship advice I ever heard was from the official of a wedding I was attending. He said, "When your spouse deserves love the least that's when you need to love them the most." That one really hit me because what he was saying was that your feelings or emotions can't determine how you choose to treat someone. If you give them only what you think they "deserve" when you're in the middle of a conflict, not only will you not help the situation, you will likely do more damage.

Often when someone's difficult or when we're frustrated with them, we withhold the one ingredient that could prove to be the cure because we don't want to reward the person. In fact, sometimes we may even want to punish them more than we want to resolve the situation. We're waiting for them to "see" what they did wrong, but that rarely happens in the moment.

Instead, we should try meeting their need…that unmet personality need that has forced them over to the dark side. It is much more likely that if you help them leave the "dark side," they'll come to their senses and acknowledge their shortcoming later. This is counterintuitive, because everything in you screams: "that won't help them see what they need to see!" But meeting their need (even the ones they don't realize they have) will help them get to a better place.

Personality types are able to function positively when those needs are met. That is when you will see their strengths in full display. But when these needs are unmet, their weaknesses become more prominent. In fact, many of the weaknesses of that personality type are really attempts—whether consciously or unconsciously—to satisfy those needs.

When it comes to leading, it is easy to talk about it from the standpoint of authority and submission. Because people are employees, there is a level of compliance that can be obtained simply through the organizational structure and the chain of command. But leadership by authority will never beat leadership by influence. With authority, you can get people to work, but with influence you increase people's effort, and there is a huge difference between work and effort.

Great leaders increase people's effort. They do this through the power of influence. But the challenge is that it takes different things to influence different personalities. When you learn what makes different people tick, you're able to truly influence and get the best out of each person. The more capable a leader is at dong that, the more engaged his team will be.

Personality Assessment:

To better understand the remainder of the book, it is recommended that you take the Force Multiplier personality assessment. The Force Multiplier personality assessment was designed to help you better understand your own strengths and opportunities for growth. The assessment is comprised of 24 questions that will help identify your personality blend. The assessment is located at www.tonychatman.com/forcemultiplier

As a thank you for purchasing the book you can take the assessment at a significantly discounted price using the discount code: FO47RC3$BO@K Please don't share this code with anyone. After using the code, you will complete a registration which will allow you to both view your results online as well as download the results whenever you need them.

One word of direction: It is very important to answer the questions not based on any situational environment (at work, at church etc.) but to answer them based on who you are at your core. This may take time and introspection, but don't worry, the assessment isn't timed nor does the amount of time it takes to complete factor into the scoring.

So, let's get going, or as my dad's best friend used to say, "Let's get on with the get on!"

Chapter 7

CONDUCTORS

The concert hall is full. There is an air of anticipation as the curtain opens. Behind the curtain is a philharmonic orchestra comprised of seasoned pros who auditioned against and beat other seasoned pros for the honor of sitting in their seats. And now, they're just sitting patiently as the audience waits. And then she arrives. The conductor. She makes her way to the podium, and all eyes turn to her. She opens the score the orchestra is to perform, picks up a baton with her right hand, and, as her hand begins to move, everyone follows, and the hall is filled with the sound of beautiful music.

Total control, that's what the conductor has, total control. She chooses the music, sets the pace, and tells everyone how loudly to play, when to change their volume, and when the piece is over. And the beauty of it is that if she's wrong, if she sets the wrong tempo or if she gives the wrong cues, it doesn't matter. Everyone still follows—no arguing, no questioning. Just following. The conductor is in complete control, and that's where she is happy. In a perfect world, that would be the life of a conductor.

Some people don't like to lead. They don't want the pressure, they don't want the responsibility, and they don't want to be in charge. Not Conductors. They don't want to be passengers, they want to drive. They need to drive. Being in charge is where they are most comfortable; it really is their comfort zone.

Conductors are leaders and doers. They want things to get done, and they want them done now. And when things don't get done fast enough or when things are getting off track, the natural response of conductors is to jump in and take over. They can't help it; it's their nature. Deep down, conductors are convinced that they not only are the best person for the job, they're convinced that their way is the only way.

Needs

As mentioned previously, each personality has a number of different needs. Personality types are able to function positively when those needs are met. That's when you will see their strengths in full display. But when those needs go unmet, their weaknesses become more prominent. In fact, many of the weaknesses of that personality type are really attempts— whether consciously or unconsciously—to satisfy those needs.

Conductors have four basic needs. The first need is control. It is primary. It's not just that they want to be in control, they know what they want done and how they want it done. They are confident in themselves. They trust themselves. Often, they believe that they know more than everyone else as well. Because of these things, conductors are not willing to leave it up to someone else to determine the outcome if the situation involves them. If they're not in control, they're not content.

The second need is power. Power is different than control. With power comes authority, and with authority people follow you and they respect you. With power, you're not only in control of events, you're in control of other people—not only what they do, but how quickly they do it. With power, you can give commands and directives that other people listen to and execute. You don't have to explain everything (that takes up precious time in which other things can get accomplished). You say it, and they do it. Yes, power is a necessity for conductors.

The third need for Conductors is respect; they actually demand it. There are a lot of things you can do to conductors that they'll let roll off their backs, but not showing respect or, even worse, disrespecting them, isn't one of them. Regardless of how they treat others, Conductors expect to be treated with respect. To them it's not a function of what they've done or not done to earn that respect; they must have it, and if they don't get it, there will be hell to pay.

The fourth need for Conductors is recognition. Conductors like and need to be recognized for all of their contributions to the team and, even more importantly, for their hard work. They're not big fans of "atta boy." They prefer money or something tangible, but acknowledging their hard work is a huge deposit in the account of conductors. One of the greatest compliments you can give a conductor is, "It's amazing how much you get done in a day." This is like gold to them.

Strengths

First of all, most Conductors are very self-motivated. The moment they know what needs to be done, they're on it. These are not people who you need to motivate and check up on. And they're not going to get tired or give up before the goal is reached; they have an internal engine that keeps them going. If there were ever a person for whom the phrase, "Get 'er done" was appropriate, it is the Conductor. They are always going, and they will not be out-worked.

Almost all Conductors are goal oriented. They love having goals. Goals drive them, stretch them, and push them. When given goals, Conductors don't just want to meet goals...they want to exceed the goals given them. Goals are motivators for them, and most Conductors have goals for every area of their lives. They have life goals, business goals, and career goals. Conductors don't just create goals, they accomplish them. They are willing to do whatever it takes to achieve their goals. Failure is not an option for them.

Almost every single Conductor I've ever met is extremely ambitious. Success is one of those things that Conductors think about continuously. To them, life is often measured by success. Their ambition drives them past where others are willing to go. They don't just want to succeed. They want to be the best, and they want to crush anyone or anything that stands in their way.

Conductors are very productive and hard-working. They're all about productivity. It drives them nuts when other people don't show a sense of urgency or a willingness and motivation to get things done.

This is very important: Conductors are very decisive. Many people, when making a decision, want a lot of information. They want to do a complete analysis of the situation—every piece of information is important to them. Not Conductors. Conductors don't want all the details. They want enough information, normally the bottom line along with any relevant risks, so that they can make a quick decision. Conductors are all about quick decisions. Remember, they're trying to accomplish a lot in the most efficient manner possible, so they don't want to waste time hearing a bunch of non-critical information. They would rather make a good and quick decision than waste time trying to perfect the decision. For them, the decision doesn't have to be perfect, as long as it's effective and timely. As one Conductor explained to the class during a workshop, anything other than the bottom line and the most important information is like static or background noise to them. They're not listening.

Conductors are not easily discouraged. In fact, one of the things that is very unique about them is that they have a high tolerance for rejection. Where rejection crushes some, it doesn't even phase the Conductor. They don't take it personally. If you've ever been out to a nightclub, which I know that no one who's reading his book has ever done, you may have seen that guy who asks everyone to dance. Un-phased by rejection, he'll go from person to person. If the situation calls for it, he'll ask three women who are not only sitting at the same table, but in the middle of a conversation with each other to dance because, in his mind, if they say no it is not that they're rejecting him, it's that they don't have a clear understanding of what they're missing out on. If they had any idea who they were talking to and the opportunity in front of them, they would have stopped what they were doing and asked *him* to dance.

Conductors are independent. They work well by themselves. They don't always have to be in teams, and they don't always need social interaction to be effective. In fact, they prefer to work alone, that way there's no one slowing them down. Give them a goal, and get out of the way.

Conductors thrive on opposition. They want to win, and when there's opposition, they don't just want to win, they want to crush the opposition. If you've ever been to a seminar where a motivational speaker says, "I had this goal and then someone told me I couldn't do it, and that just motivated me to do it even more," that person was almost certainly a Conductor. There are plenty of other people that if you tell him something is impossible they might think, "Hey maybe you're right, maybe that's not what I should be doing with my life."   But not a conductor. That opposition is just what they needed to ensure the goal would be achieved. In fact, if you ever want to motivate a Conductor, tell them that something is difficult, that most people could not do it, or that it's impossible. They're not having that. They will give every last ounce of their energy to prove you wrong.

A Brief Observation

Historically. the personality types have not been treated equally in the workplace. Of the personality types in the workplace, Conductors have been the most highly valued. Whether in the public or private sector, the military, nonprofit organizations, religious organizations, or philanthropic organizations, it doesn't matter because the Conductor was always the one people wanted. The reason is simple: they get a lot done and are self-motivated.

This is especially true in leadership positions. Organizations have historically wanted Conductors. It's even likely that, if you've ever had to assume a leadership position, someone may have even tried to make you more like a Conductor because that was their view of what a good leader is.

But now things have changed. The workplace is no longer dependent only upon individuals accomplishing work primarily by their manual labor. Customer service and creativity dominate the workplace. Work must be done in teams for organizations to be successful. Because of this, companies now realize that every personality type is not only valued, but their contributions are critical in all levels of leadership for organizations to be successful.

The reality is, even though each personality type brings a lot of positive characteristics to the table, they each also have areas in which they need to improve. These are the things that make them difficult and can be their Achilles' heel…the very thing that keeps them from being successful.

What Makes Conductors Difficult

I've heard many experts describe Conductors as natural leaders. Conductors naturally want to lead, but that does not mean they're naturally good at it. They naturally assume the position of leadership because they value being leaders far more than they value following. In fact, one of their flaws is that they try to take the reins of leadership when that's not their role.

As mentioned previously, Conductors are control freaks, and I mean in the worst way. The minute things don't go the way they want them to, or the minute there's an opportunity for control, they step right in. Like Alexander Haig saying, "I'm in charge" after the Ronald Reagan assassination attempt (when Alexander Hague was not the next in line in the succession of power), Conductors jump in and assume control of situations regardless of whether that is their role.

An example of this occurred recently. I was scheduled to be in a meeting, and 15 minutes before the meeting I received an email from one of the people in the group who happened to be a Conductor. The email contained an agenda of the meeting. When the meeting began, he proceeded to pull out a timer (literally) and began timing everyone as they spoke to ensure that they stayed on track, because in his mind the meetings had become ineffective. Of course, he did this for everyone except himself. But there was one problem—it wasn't his meeting! The leader of the meeting just sat there stunned, mouth wide open, and unfortunately did nothing to take back control over his meeting, so we all just painfully suffered through it.

I've seen this type of scenario play out time and time again. Within a team or a small organization, there can be Conductors who have assumed control of a group in which they have no authority. This often happens when the Conductor perceives there is no leadership or leadership is weak or ineffective. I've even seen situations where the Conductor's manager or the organization's upper management was too intimidated by the Conductor to step in and right the situation.

It is the Conductors' controlling nature that often leads to micromanaging. Conductors have a hard time letting go. The thought of delegating to someone else is unbearable for Conductors. Even though they know they need to, they just can't seem to hand something off and stay out of the way.

Instead, they pressure people to agree with their unattainable expectations, micromanage them through the entire process, and then blame them when success is not achieved. What Conductors don't realize is that their micromanaging is undermining the success that they so desire. By micromanaging, they're often interrupting the work that is being done. And often they completely demotivate the people that they've delegated work to.

Most Conductors really hate when the people they manage want to telework. The thought of not being able to see someone and monitor their day is unbearable. The belief that if someone is not within eyesight and might be slacking off often makes the conductor reject the idea of teleworking. The Conductor would much rather have everybody together so they can see them, micromanage them, and be certain they're getting every possible ounce of work out from them.

Conductors can also be very impatient. Because they're all about getting things done, they hate anything that gets in the way of their moving quickly. Whether that is the need to collaborate and brainstorm, the need to have a constructive conversation, or even the need to calculate the potential problems with the plan, Conductors look at these things as nothing but hindrances that are slowing them down. Whether they say it overtly, you hear it in a condescending tone, or you see it in the rolling of their eyes when things aren't moving fast enough, they make it clear that the contributions being made are more of a hindrance than a help.

Conductors are obsessed with success and winning. They must be the best, they have to be first, and they must win at all costs. Many Conductors will circumvent rules and regulations just to make sure they win, and some will even sabotage the efforts of those they view as competition. This desire to win is not just limited to performance. The desire is to win every disagreement, every argument, and every confrontation. Winning is everything; defeat is unacceptable.

This desire to win translates into Conductors becoming workaholics. They will push and push and push, sometimes even sending themselves to an early grave. The problem is not just that *they* are workaholics and killing themselves, it's that they expect everyone around them to be workaholics as well. They look down on people who leave work early or who desire a work-life balance. They want everyone to push just as hard as they do because when others work hard, it contributes to the Conductor's success.

And by far, the biggest issue with Conductors is that they can resort to bullying. Whether it is through physical intimidation, threatening, overexertion of authority, or just verbal abuse, Conductors can often function as bullies. The bigger problem is that often they get away with it for two primary reasons:

1.   In general, Conductors are great producers. So, when employees complain about a Conductor's tactics, upper management often responds with, "That's just employees complaining about having to work hard!" Even worse, upper management realizes that the Conductor has a growing problem, but they're faced with the reality that the Conductor gets results. And organizations don't want to lose that productivity.

2.   Conductors often have very strong personalities. That can be intimidating, even to seasoned executives. I've personally seen senior vice presidents who are afraid of the Conductors who were two levels below them because of their strong personality. These executives were conflict avoiders so they let them run amok, and in the process they lost their best people.

How to Work With Conductors

Conductors are very direct when talking about issues. Although some people may view that as blunt, Conductors view it as not wasting time and getting to the point. Conductors view themselves as problem solvers. When there is an issue, they jump right in. They don't mind taking risks or making decisions, especially in a crisis. What they really want is for someone give them a situation and let them run with it.

When working with Conductors, the first thing to do is to get to the point. I can't emphasize this enough. Conductors really aren't big on small talk in general, a little bit of small talk is okay, but it really needs to be only a little bit. And the more urgent the situation, the more small talk becomes inapplicable.

Normally when giving information to Conductors, you want to focus on the bottom line. They want a clear understanding of what it is expected of them and what is the overall goal. Once that's done, they're good to go. At that point, giving extra details, although seemingly helpful, is actually detrimental. The more you talk, the less clear the goal is. They really want to know what the expectations are and what role they play in it. More information just clouds the communication that is taking place. For most Conductors, once they know what to do, they stop listening anyway. At that point, their thoughts have already turned to how they are going to accomplish the goal.

I was speaking to a project manager who was working for a Conductor. She just had her performance review and was upset by the feedback she received. Although she received good overall ratings, the one piece of corrective feedback she had received was that she hadn't kept her boss up to date on a number of projects she was responsible for. This frustrated her. She had consistently updated her boss via email and kept a record of those updates. In fact, she had just updated him on all of the ongoing projects the previous week.

I asked to see one of her emails. Once I saw it, I immediately knew what was wrong. It was very detailed, thorough, and complete; full of dense paragraphs detailing the status of each project. Just what she thought he wanted. I told her, "He never read the email." She said, "What do you mean?" I told her, "The email is too long and there was no way that he read it." I knew based on our previous discussion that she was reporting to a Conductor, a Conductor with a lot of responsibility. When he said he wanted to be updated on projects, he wanted to know if they were on time, on budget, and if there were any big issues. That's it. That's all. That's not what she gave him. She gave him the details, and he would have to sift through all of those details to find what he needed. That's not going to happen. He just looked at it and moved to the next thing on his plate.

I then suggested that her next email begin with a brief introduction (a sentence or two) followed by the most pertinent information in a prioritized bulleted list. Below that she could include the details if she wanted, but I did tell her that it most likely wasn't necessary unless there was a major change in the status of a project or a previously unforeseen problem arose. After a bit of going back and forth because she needed convincing that she didn't really need all of those details, she tried it and, as expected, her boss was happy.

Also, when working with Conductors, don't get caught up in emotions and feelings. Especially in the work environment, these things are of less importance to a Conductor than being productive and effective. Normally if a conductor asks, "How are you doing?" they don't want a detailed breakdown of your current emotional state. So, don't give a synopsis of everything going on in your life, a few positive highlights will do. Notice, I said positive highlights. They aren't necessarily trying to get involved in your emotional condition.

Conductors like rewards that are tangible, things like money and plaques. Okay, yeah doesn't everybody? Yes, but for Conductors, they carry far more weight than verbal recognition. Some really like to be acknowledged in front of their peers. Conductors are far more concerned with tangible things or things that accelerate their career path.

Remember that Conductors are very assertive, specific, and direct. In an ideal situation, they want to provide direction and leadership. When the group is indecisive, they will push the team towards decisions. They welcome challenges without fear and are willing to accept the risk.

Ways to Make Deposits with Conductors

Flexibility

Allowing individuals the freedom to find their own unique ways to accomplish tasks and solve problems when appropriate.

Loyalty

Having faithful allegiance and constant support.

Clearly defined expectations

Stating verbally and in written form what you expect the organization, teams. and individuals to achieve. Expectations should be Specific, Measurable, Attainable, Realistic, and given a Timeframe (SMART).

Dealing with tough situations

Showing emotional stability, integrity (honesty), and willingness to get others involved to address a difficult situation.

Ways to Make Withdrawals with Conductors

Usurping authority

Showing disregard for established authority through open criticism or secretly doing things that go against the authority.

Passive/Aggressive

Indirectly resisting to avoid conflict; examples include procrastination, sabotage, phrasing an objection in a sarcastic or rhetorical manner.

Consistent communication/Effective communication

Using the various communication vehicles available to convey information on a regular basis.

Did you see it? The last withdrawal for Conductors is actually a deposit for other personalities. This is part of the challenge for the different personalities. Just because something would be a deposit for you does not make it a deposit for everyone.

Chapter 8

MC

There are those who love to work in the background. They don't want all the fanfare; they don't want the attention. They just want to help make whatever is being worked on a success without drawing attention to themselves. The bright lights are not for them; they'd rather work behind the scenes. MCs are not those people. MCs are built for the stage. They thrive in the spotlight. Where attention and especially attention from crowds makes some nervous and insecure, this is the place where MCs shine.

Whether a circus, awards ceremony, talent show, or other public performance, there is often one person out front who keeps things moving. They provide the transition from act to act and in many ways end up becoming the focal point of the entire show. That is the Master of Ceremonies or MC. Although the MC's primary role is to keep the event flowing and act as a bridge between segments of the event, the MC must have personality. It's not just what they do that makes MCs important, it's how they do it. The MC ensures that the audience is engaged and having fun while keeping their interest. The MC is as much entertainer as host. The one thing that a successful show can never have is a boring MC.

If you've ever hosted an event, one thing you can be sure of—things never go as planned. There is always a monkey wrench thrown into the plan. Someone arrives late or the show is behind schedule. Sometimes it's a medical emergency or a last-minute change; but, one thing is certain, barring a catastrophic event, the show must go on, and the MC has to be flexible enough to handle whatever is thrown their way. They have to be fast on their feet because when things go awry, they're going to have to improvise and do it in such a way that the average person has no idea that what just happened wasn't planned. And they have to do all of this while keeping the attention of hundreds and sometimes thousands. You have to be able to ad-lib if you're going to be a great MC.

Needs

MCs first need is attention. MCs are used to being in the spotlight. They were built for it. The center of attention is the center of their comfort zone. It's important not to judge the MC because of this need. It's easy to think of this need as being superficial or narcissistic. Attention is to an MC what order is to a Navigator, what peace is to a diplomat, and what control is to a conductor. This means that MCs often need to look externally to get their most primary need met. Because attention is so critical for MCs, when they don't have it they will do things either consciously or unconsciously to draw the attention back where it should be...on themselves.

MCs also look for approval from other people. Being accepted is critical to an MC; they thrive on it. It is necessary both for their survival and for them to function in a positive way. Here is how important praise is for MCs: you've probably heard it said from a leadership expert or some authority figure that, "It is more important to be respected than to be liked." This is not true for MCs. For them, being liked trumps being respected. Of course, they would love to have both, but their aim in a relationship is to be liked and have fun more than it is to be respected.

Praise is another important need for an MC. Praise is different than recognition. Recognition is an acknowledgement of one's efforts. It can be verbal or in the form of rewards. Whereas recognition acknowledges one's contribution, praise shows an actual appreciation for the contribution of the person or of the person themselves. Although it sounds like a minor difference, it's actually a big deal when applied to MCs. Praise connects on a deeper and more emotional level than recognition. When giving praise to an MC, you are transferring positive emotions to them. It's like connecting an IV of positivity into their system.

Which brings me to the MCs next need: they need to have fun. Whether at work or in life, fun is a necessity for them. They will take breaks and do whatever it takes to refill their fun quota. In fact, many MCs will be criticized for not growing up and for not taking certain aspects of life more seriously. What others don't realize is growing up was never the goal.

Strengths

The first strength of an MC is that they are great talkers. They are never at a loss for words. Their storytelling ability is impeccable. They are fantastic oral communicators whether

one-on-one or in front of a larger audience. They are able to
come up with just the right word at the right time and they do
it effortlessly. And it's normally spontaneous, they don't need
a script nor do they need to think through everything ahead
of time. Most successful MCs have learned to leverage their
ability to communicate to be more successful in their careers.

MCs are extremely social; in fact, they're often the life of
the party. They can just walk into a room and light the room
up with their presence. It's like they've never met a stranger.
They start conversations; they engage with everyone around
them; they float around the room like social butterflies
making sure that everyone is having a great time. They love
the energy, and being around more people energizes them.

MCs love people. In fact, MCs are by definition
extroverted. When thinking of introversion and extroversion,
people often think in terms of behavior. They think of
extroverts as loud and boisterous and introverts as shy and
quiet. A better way of think of introversion and extroversion
is to ask yourself: "Does interacting with others energize
you or does it drain you?" For extroverts, social interaction
energizes them; for introverts, it drains them. MCs are
extroverts, they need social interaction. It's what keeps them
going and when they don't have it, they'll either go looking
for it or risk getting depressed and discouraged.

MCs are extremely enthusiastic. I've used the word
energetic a few times to describe them, this was not done
by mistake. It's easy to underestimate just how energetic
they really are. Often, they have enough energy for two or

three people. Everything they do, they do with vigor and pep. Their energy can be overwhelming at times for those who are unprepared. That energy also seeps into how they communicate. They communicate with an infectious zeal. They passionately engage people during conversation, and often they're able to transfer their energy to other people.

MCs in general are improvisers. This is very important to understand. Most MCs feel that they work best when they have the freedom to "play it by ear." MCs are very talented and most at home in the moment. They often reject the constrictions of plans, to-do lists, or calendars. This allows MCs to work well in fast-moving environments. They're extremely flexible and as things change they quickly adapt to the new situation. In fact, they often get bored if things don't move fast enough or become too routine. One of the worst things you could do is put an MC in a cubicle with a computer screen and a phone and say, "Do this routine over and over again for 40 hours a week." Lives would be in danger.

MCs are very creative. There are times when you're in a meeting and you hear some executive say, "We need to start thinking outside the box." Don't do this! That's not what they really want. Rarely do people want others to think outside of the box. They may want you to think further away from the center of the box, but boxes are there for a reason. They allow for consistency and repeatability. Stay away from the edges, there's danger out there. But for some MCs, outside of the box is where they live. It's one thing to think outside of the box. It's a whole different animal when you have someone who doesn't see a box. That's when everything is fair game.

Creativity is not restrained by the limits of previously held beliefs or social norms. Many MCs are creative all the time. They can't shut it off. They may not share all of it with you, but new ideas are always flowing through their minds. Not all those ideas will be good. Some will be horrible, some sound stupid, and others will be impossible to execute. But every once in a while, they'll come up with an amazing find that could change the future of an organization. MCs are often a one-person brainstorming session.

MCs are quick to volunteer for new jobs and responsibilities. When no one else is willing to step up, they are. In fact, they're delighted to be the ones. They not only volunteer for new responsibilities, they think of new activities as well. When you're constantly thinking of new ways for things to be done, you're also thinking of new things that need to be done.

One of MCs' strongest strengths is their great sense of humor. They're great at telling jokes and their timing is impeccable. Whether planned or spontaneous, MCs enjoy bringing levity to a tense situation.

What Makes MCs Difficult

One thing important thing I've learned over the years is that a strength, when it is unbridled and out of control, can become a weakness! One of the MC's greatest strengths is their ability to talk. They are often known for it. One of their greatest weaknesses is their ability to talk. They show no restraint when it comes to talking. They can talk too much and at the wrong time. At work, MCs are the ones who go from cubicle to cubicle looking for someone to talk to while others are trying to get work done. They're the ones who always have something cute to say in a meeting, and they often try to get in the last word. They often talk too much.

Most MCs are very disorganized. It has to do with how they process information. The more creative you are, the more you think outside the box. Boxes produce consistency and reliability. They help us stay organized. If you look at an MC's workspace, it is normally very disorganized. Their homes are often disorganized as well. The common areas, the rooms in which they entertain may be clean, but I assure you, if you get the chance to look into the "off limit rooms" you will see chaos. What may be amazing to you is that although there appears to be no rhyme or reason to their mess, they often have no problem finding things when they need them.

MCs can be narcissistic. They often become consumed with themselves. In conversation, they'll interrupt constantly, and, if the conversation isn't about them, they will jump in with some pseudo relevant piece of information to draw attention back to themselves. They'll always get some word in because it would kill them to be left out. They may or may not realize it, but they really are striving to be the center of every situation.

They don't just want attention, they want everyone to like them. And they go to great lengths to try and get people to like them. Remember the *Winnie The Pooh* (Methuen, England,

1926; and E.P. Dutton, U.S., 1926) character Tigger? He is the ultimate example of an MC. The less attention you pay to him, the more in your face he becomes. You just can't ignore him. Often it's their very effort to be liked that pushes people away. The harder they try to be liked, the more they get on people's nerves. A friend recently said of an MC, "What bugs me about him is that he tries so hard to be liked. It really bugs me."

Most MCs exaggerate. Sometimes they're completely aware of it, other times it just flows out in the moment. It can be with data or it can be the details of the story to make it sound far more exciting than it really is. Normally the exaggeration is either for effect or part of an excuse. Facts aren't the most important ingredient in a conversation for MCs. They are fine with disregarding the facts for the sake of impact.

Most MCs are easily distracted. They have a hard time staying focused on one thing. It's especially easy for them to be visually distracted. This can be a big problem. Earlier I said that they volunteer for jobs and responsibilities. The problem is that they often over commit! Because they love approval, it's hard for MCs to say no. So, they quickly commit without thinking through whether or not they can actually accomplish what they're signing up for. Even if they don't overcommit, because they're disorganized and easily distracted, they rarely come through with what they committed to do. They have very little follow-through. They're great starters, but poor finishers.

MCs can be very emotional. Often their first reaction to news is an over-reaction. Whether they are overjoyed by great news or angry and upset due to bad news, their reactions, or at least their initial reactions, are usually out of proportion with the situation. This makes their day an emotional rollercoaster. Really up, really down, but rarely in the middle.

Finally, MCs don't like to plan or prepare. They're improvisors, remember? They'd rather wing it, that's where they're most comfortable. This can be especially troublesome when they are working in teams. While others are charting a course, the MCs are doing their own thing.

How to Work with MCs

Remember, MCs really enjoy talking to and communicating with others. It energizes them. They are very enthusiastic and optimistic in a way that can be infectious and persuasive.

When working with MCs, the first thing to do is give them a chance to socialize. Build it into their day. MCs are by definition extroverted and social interaction energizes and revitalizes them. Once they have those social breaks, you'll be amazed at what they can accomplish with all that energy and vigor they have.

One mistake people often make when working with MCs is that they try to rush talk time by cutting them off and "getting to the point." This ends up being counterproductive. They don't get the point, nor do they take the hint. What this actually ends up doing is prolonging the conversation. Often people will find that they spent more time trying to get the

MC to stop talking than they would have if they just let them talk in the first place.

Give MCs important information in writing. There are two reasons for this. First, most MCs process information visually. Words make more sense to them when they can picture what's going on. Pictures and charts are far more effective in communicating ideas than words and data. If they can see it, they can probably do it.

Second, as mentioned earlier, MCs often over commit. What is interesting is that at times they not only overcommit, but, because they are disorganized, it is unlikely that they've kept any record of what they've committed to. In fact, it is not uncommon for MCs to forget that they ever made a commitment in the first place (I'm not kidding, this really does happen - a lot!). This is especially important when dealing with a lot of details. MCs are not naturally detail-oriented people, so when discussing details, they'll often drift off mentally. Following up a conversation with a quick summary of action items can be very valuable when working with an MC.

Reinforce positive behavior with rewards and recognition. Positive reinforcement is critical for MCs. In reality, it is important for everyone, but it is especially important to MCs. MCs don't respond or change because of discipline or threats. In fact, children with an MC personality often won't mature and develop without positive reinforcement. Rewards and recognition are the primary motivator for MCs.

It is important to provide MCs with some structure and accountability. Even though they prefer to work without a calendar or to-do list, some structure makes them more effective. It keeps them from over-promising and under-delivering. Don't provide too much structure and don't micromanage them, even though you'll be tempted to. You can balance the structure with social time or fun activities. MCs will most likely fight structure, but in the end it will be for their benefit.

MCs are creative problem-solvers. They're motivators and communicators who are good at working with the team to accomplish goals. They have a good sense of humor and like to create a comfortable environment for the team.

Ways to Make Deposits with MCs

Involving others in decision making

Pulling in associates, letting them take part in the decision-making process. This also includes hearing their suggestions even if their suggestions don't influence the outcome.

Giving recognition for a job well done

Giving praise when people achieve something or go above and beyond what is expected or the call of duty.

Knowing the individual

Taking the time to know co-workers on an individual level. Not necessarily being "best buds," but getting to know them as a person.

Flexibility

Allowing individuals the freedom to find their own unique ways to accomplish tasks and solve problems when appropriate.

Ways to Make Withdrawals with MCs

Failing to give recognition

Omitting praise when people achieve something; failing to plan celebrations for major accomplishments.

Predictability/Consistency

Exhibiting the same behavior and responses to similar situations.

Clearly defined expectations

Stating verbally and in written form what you expect the organization, teams, and individuals to achieve. Expectations should be Specific, Measurable, Attainable, Realistic, and given a Timeframe (SMART).

Chapter 9

DIPLOMATS

Another international incident occurred that prompted growing hostility between nations. International conflict seems inescapable. Troops and resources are being moved to areas that will likely make up the battleground between two opposing factions. Each nation decides to make one last ditch effort before the inevitable happens. Each nation sends representatives to a neutral meeting place to see if there is any chance of resolution. As the meeting begins, each representative expresses both the needs of their nation and an understanding of the need for peaceful relations between the two governments. After multiple meetings and discussions on issues, policies, and positions, negotiations end and a treaty is reached. Once again, the work of the Diplomats has helped nations avoid war.

Advocating for international cooperation in remote locations is often difficult and rarely receives the recognition that it warrants. When there is a need to either build or smooth relations between countries, especially in the highly sensitive areas of politics and trade, the diplomat is the one you count on. Whether it's attending international dinners or assisting in the development of foreign policy, Diplomats discharge all their duties with a demeanor that ensures a positive relationship between their country of residence and their home nation. Their ability to build political capital with others increases their influence and allows their country to maintain diplomatic relations and minimizes the threat of war.

In the same way, those with the Diplomat personality are master relationship builders. Without agenda, they show a genuine concern for others, making the type of deposits that not only build trust, but loyalty and commitment as well. The type of commitment that later can be called upon during times of need. Diplomats go through life building powerful networks of relationships and have a reputation for being dependable and trustworthy. Whether they realize it or not, Diplomats are never alone—they always have allies, whether hidden or in plain sight.

Needs

Critical to a Diplomat is peace. In fact, peace is one of the most important things you can understand about Diplomats. Now when I say peace, I don't mean "peace on earth!" I mean peace around them. "Can't we all just get along?" When Diplomats are at peace, they are able to be in their comfort zone. And when peace is disrupted, most Diplomats will almost reflexively do things to move back to a state of peace. Many of the Diplomat's greatest weaknesses revolve around their need to keep peace at all times and at all costs.

Trust is also essential for Diplomats. Diplomats prefer to build trust with you so that they can more closely work with you. That being said, based on many conversations I've had with Diplomats, most will only work with you on a limited basis until trust has been established. That means there's only so much information they're going to give you, only so much of a benefit of the doubt they'll give you, and only so much they're willing to do for you until trust has been firmly established. When people take the time to build trust with Diplomats, they find an ally who is willing to put their reputation on the line, but this takes time. And if you ever do anything to violate the trust that has been built, game over! It is nearly impossible to fix a relationship with a Diplomat once trust is damaged.

Another need for Diplomats is self-worth. Where self-esteem is often linked to what a person accomplishes, self-worth is a function of how a person feels about themselves or their own value. Self-worth is about who you are more than what you do. Diplomats want to wake up in the morning, look in the mirror, and be happy with who they see. Because of this, it is critical for Diplomats to stay true to themselves. That means there are lines they just won't cross. When a Diplomat loses the ability to see value within themselves, bad things happen.

Strengths

One of the greatest strengths of Diplomats is their empathy. Empathy is the ability to see something from another person's perspective—the ability to "walk in someone else's shoes." Diplomats excel not only in their ability to feel empathy, they have an uncanny ability to express empathy to others as well. They seem to know the right thing to say and the right way to say it no matter what the situation. They also know when the best thing to do is to say nothing and just be there for the other person.

Where some go to workshops to learn how to both be empathetic as well as how to express empathy, Diplomats do this naturally. It's one of the things that allows them to be so effective when relating to others. This makes them the people you want to be around when you are overwhelmed or despondent. They have an almost unnatural ability to help people get through the most upsetting situations. Diplomats are hardwired to always be in tune with other people's emotions in order to be connected. It's as though they have a radar built inside of them that detects the emotions of those around them. And it's always on; they can't shut it off.

This ability to be empathic, combined with their natural inclination to be sympathetic and concerned for other people, gives them amazing influence. They want to be there for others, to help them when they're in need. They are constantly building trust, loyalty, and commitment with people around them. And it happens naturally. They are concerned about the best interests of everyone else. And people know that the Diplomat would never intentionally do anything to harm them.

Often in an organization, you have people in a leadership positions, and you have what I call opinion leaders. Opinion leaders are the ones people really go to for input and perspective. When new direction is given, it is often vetted through the eyes of the opinion leader. And they normally hold more influence over the group than the manager. They have made so many deposits with people that people naturally follow the diplomat. They've built social capital with others, and they're very wise in how they spend it.

Because they've built so much trust, Diplomats are also aware of what's really going on around the office and how people are really doing. They don't gossip (that would be a betrayal of trust), so people confide in them. People seek them out for advice. They share information with them knowing that what is said will be held in the strictest of confidence. This information is extremely valuable when extinguishing conflict due to others not knowing the whole story and making assumptions.

Diplomats are temperate. Temperate is one of those ideas that is often misunderstood as well as undervalued. When I say temperate, I mean they don't overreact emotionally, even under stress. Some, like conductors, tend to get angry when under stress. Others, like MCs, tend to overreact to events when under stress. Not diplomats. Even under stress, they don't get too up when they receive good news, and they don't get too down when the news is bad. They always stay within a nice little range. They're consistent.

Diplomats are amazing mediators. Their empathy allows them to help both sides see the other's perspective. They're able do this without offending either party. This allows them to help everyone find common ground.

Diplomats are also great listeners. During a conversation, they don't just listen to what is said, but they're naturally in tune with the tone and the body language behind the words. They hear what you feel and what you meant as well as what you said. And amazingly, they're also quite aware of what you didn't say as well as the implications of that.

Diplomats are naturally collaborative. They're great at pulling other people in. They don't want all of the glory, nor do they want to do things by themselves. They don't prefer to lead by being upfront or by authority, but by leveraging the different personalities of the people around them. They go out of their way to make sure that everyone is involved and that everyone's voices have been heard.

Diplomats are consistent almost to the point of being predictable. You always know what you're getting with diplomats. They're consistent in their work.

Diplomats are agreeable. They are easy to get along with. They're not going to rock the boat. When in conflict, if they decide it's just not worth the fight, they'll just move on. It's more important to them to get along than to win the argument. But don't confuse their agreeability with buy-in. They may have reservations, but unless the repercussions are big enough or they have been ignored for a period of time, they won't worry about it. They'll go along to get along.

What Makes Diplomats Difficult

First and foremost, Diplomats avoid conflict. Diplomats are great during times of peace, but they're really not built for war. When other people are in conflict, they don't want to get involved. They want no part of it. Conflict disrupts their peace, so they avoid it at all costs. They'll also avoid giving bad news and sometimes even corrective feedback because they don't want to hurt anyone. When the situation turns into true conflict, they often disappear hoping that over time it will all blow over. And when they do get involved, they want it to be over as quickly as possible.

They also avoid conflict which involves themselves. Diplomats have a tendency to give in quickly. When they're a part of a conflict, they will often yield to the other person's wishes or demands. Again, this does not mean that they're in any way resolved, they just don't feel that the fight is worth it. They value the relationship more than being right. So, they tell themselves that by sucking it up, they're being the bigger person, they're taking the high road.

The problem is that a person can only suck it up for so long. At some point, there will be a boundary that they are not willing to cross, and they'll stand their ground. Or, if they have been pushed around too much, or have given in too many times without anyone considering them, they'll hit their limit and like a pressure cooker they blow. And it's never a pretty sight. It seems to come out of nowhere. And usually at that point, whatever you are in conflict about is not the real issue. It's the buildup of all the other things that happen before that's causing the blow up.

Diplomats resist change. Like I said before, Diplomats are steady and consistent. Change will disrupt their habits. Plus, people lose their minds during times of change. And dealing with those people will certainly mess up their peace.

Diplomats can be too sympathetic. There are times when people need a shoulder to cry on, but there are other times when people need a good swift kick in the pants. They're wrong, and they need to take responsibility for their mistake. Unfortunately for most Diplomats, empathy and sympathy are the only tools in their belts. So, it's the solution they implement for all of a person's ills.

Diplomats are not known for being assertive. They're far more suggestive and nuanced in conversation than direct. They would much rather hint or suggest a want or need than outright say it. That could be come across as rude, and they don't want to do that. This can lead to them using a passive aggressive style of communication when they want something done.

In general, Diplomats are steady, stable workers who take ownership of their projects and take pride in doing a great job. They are great team players who will often forfeit their needs to the needs of the team. They're understanding and friendly to coworkers and are great listeners. They're pretty predictable in their actions.

How to Work with Diplomats

When leading or working with a Diplomat, first and foremost it's important get to know them as a person. I'm not saying you have to become their best friend, but a personal relationship is a must for connecting with and working with Diplomats. This can't just be something you check-off of your to-do-list; make sure you're sincerely trying to get to know them. This means, don't try to cut this time short or make it a "formal meeting" as neither will be effective. It has to be a sincere relationship. And remember, they're more likely than any other personality to be able to tell when you're insincere. If you build this relationship, you'll not only have a great associate, but a powerful ally who has a lot of social/political capital.

Diplomats need crystal clear directions and expectations to be effective. They don't want to guess or try and figure out what you want, they want specific direction on what needs to be done and how it should be done. They do want to give input, but they really need to know the goal, how it should be done, and how they will be evaluated when it's all over.

Expect that it may take some time for Diplomats to adjust to and embrace change. For most Diplomats, adapting to a new situation can be particularly challenging. Give them the situation in a non-threatening manner, and then give them some time to process that information. This is very important as you want the Diplomat to buy in to the idea, if not they may be agreeable and they may nod-their heads in agreement, but that in no way means you have buy in.

Early on in my career, I learned a valuable lesson about working with Diplomats especially during change. I was a new manager, and as I was working with my team, I noticed that there was one person, we'll call him Tom, who had been there longer than I. Most people really liked Tom, and those who didn't at least respected him. Everyone went to Tom for direction and input. This frustrated me. I thought to myself, "Hey, I'm the manager, they should all be coming to me, not

Tom." I began to view Tom as more of a threat than an asset. I didn't realize it then, but the real issue wasn't Tom, it was my insecurity.

One fateful day, when the team was in the middle of a pretty big procedural change, I went to Tom to get his viewpoint on the situation. I knew that people weren't buying into this change, and I was getting frustrated. I knew that he had his finger on the pulse of the group and really wanted his perspective. Tom began to share a couple of minor concerns he had with me about the change (I think he was testing the water to see how receptive I really was). I thanked Tom for his input, thought about it for a brief time, and then I implemented exactly what he had shared with me.

What happened next was nothing short of magic for me. Not only did Tom's suggestions work, but Tom began to give me more ideas and concerns. He helped me to see the perspective of those who had to implement this change in a way I hadn't considered. He then pointed out some of the pitfalls along with potential solutions (he was quick to give credit to the sources of these insights) and even recommended having me talk to a few particular people who could give me ideas on how to make the changes work more effectively and still make the majority happy. He was putting me in a situation where everyone could win.

Over time, Tom became a trusted resource. Not only was he willing to share his perspective, but once he felt good about the change, I often used him as the spokesperson to introduce change. The way people responded to Tom was amazing. He had built up so many deposits that having his seal of approval on an idea almost insured immediate buy in. I was very careful to keep Tom and his reputation protected. If he wasn't bought in, but it was still something that had to be done, I kept him out of it and he appreciated it. Working with Tom taught me how to leverage the power of my opinion leaders.

Diplomats in general are reliable and dependable. They are loyal team players who prefer to follow the rules. Diplomats are good listeners, they are patient, and can help resolve conflicts. They are focused and have a good sense of people and relationships. They are even-tempered and provide stability on the team. They're patient, realistic, and practical.

Ways to Make Deposits with Diplomats

Knowing the individual

Taking the time to know co-workers on an individual level. Not necessarily being "best buds," but getting to know them as a person.

Honesty/Openness

Consistently expressing the facts, even about difficult news, and sharing your feelings about that news.

Build trust

Identifying what makes people believe that you are reliable, honest, and willing to advocate for them and then taking steps consistently to exhibit those qualities in your interactions with everyone.

Predictability/Consistency

Exhibiting the same behavior and responses to similar situations.

Ways to Make Withdrawals with Diplomats

Playing favorites

Consciously or unconsciously showing preference for certain people. This behavior is demonstrated by amount of time spent with certain people, opportunities that are granted only to certain people, and recognition and praise that is only given to certain people.

Too busy for others

Having the appearance of being unavailable or stating one's lack of availability.

Unnecessary conflict/stress

Using conflict or stress as a management tool. Playing Devil's Advocate.

Chapter 10

NAVIGATORS

There are those who in both life and business always seem to have a plan. Before they ever move into action, they've thought out every little detail. They've planned and prepared for every conceivable obstacle. They not only have a well-thought out plan, they have a strategy for successfully executing that plan. For them, nothing happens without a plan. In fact, just the thought of shooting from the hip and not knowing where they're going or what's the end goal is appalling to them. If they can't have a plan so that they can do it right the first time, they'd rather not do it all. These are the Navigators.

Long before the advent of global positioning satellites, sailors needed someone who would be trusted with the responsibility of charting out the ship's course. As the captain had to be concerned with the overall mission of the ship, the boat's seaworthiness and condition as well as the crew, the Navigator's primary responsibilities was to be aware of the ship's position at all times, especially with respect to their intended destination. The Navigator maintained the ship's nautical charts and navigational equipment and was aware not only of the best overall route, but of the hazards that the ship and crew could potentially run into on the journey. The Navigator was a planner, a planner whose accuracy would likely determine the outcome of the mission.

The Navigator personality type is the same way. They are planners. They are intent on mapping out a direction and strategy to accomplish whatever lies before them. And don't expect them to get going until they completely understand what is expected of them and where they are going. They're not going to "wing it" or "fly by the seat of their pants."

Navigators function as your team's GPS. In a group, they see themselves as the one who needs to keep everyone and everything on track. When they're asking questions, reminding people of deadlines, or holding others accountable, they're just doing their job (even if it's not really their responsibility or they're not at work). Many of the actions you see your Navigator boss or coworkers doing is just them trying to navigate.

Often you will hear a CEO or some other executives say to their organization, "We need to start thinking outside the box." Although there are a group of Navigators that are extremely creative, it's good to remember that the Navigators are the ones that built the box in the first place. Navigators play by the rules. They understand that the rules are there for a reason. Rules are there to protect us from danger. Rules also ensure consistency. Don't expect Navigators to bend the rules. They not only believe in the rules, they protect the rules and often act as sentries making sure that others abide by the rules as well.

Needs

Of all the needs a Navigator may have, the number one, and by far the most important, is accuracy. Accuracy is primary.

Whether it is making decisions, working with information, or just getting an update on a situation, for Navigators, accuracy is always the first concern. I know that all of us want accurate information, but for Navigators it's different. Everything is based first on accuracy. It is from this foundation of accuracy the Navigators are able to do other things, but they know that if the information that they're dealing with is not accurate and that information they're giving to others is not accurate, everything they try to do afterward will be flawed.

For Navigators, accuracy is not only important when receiving information, it is important when giving information as well. Navigators will go through great lengths to make sure that any information they give is as close to perfect as you can possibly get. This means that, sometimes, there will be delays because for Navigators, accuracy is more important than speed. They will slow things down to first make sure things are right regardless of all the other needs.

Another important need for Navigators is order. In the most basic sense, order is that point where people and things are arranged in a way that makes logical sense. For Navigators, order is what allows them to locate things in the most effective way. Order increases efficiency. Order is what allows for a clear vision and mission. Order is what allows people to know their roles. Order is what enables people to create definitive strategies to reach their goals. For Navigators, order is a must.

If there are two things Navigators hate (and trust me, there are more than two things that they hate), they are chaos and ambiguity. Chaos, a lack of order, brings confusion. It is actually defined by Merriam Webster as a state of things in which chance is supreme. To a Navigator, that thought is about as appealing as chewing aluminum foil.

Ambiguity is fatal to a Navigator. The thought that a situation can be left to interpretation or that there isn't one single meaning or interpretation can drive Navigators nuts. Navigators avoid these two conditions as though they were the plague.

The other big need of Navigators is perfection. Perfection is different than accuracy; perfection is being free from having flaw or fault. Although Navigators want accuracy, the end goal for them is perfection. In all honesty everyone wants perfection, but for Navigators it is far beyond a want. It is a need. A need that drives them.

Perfection is always the goal; it's what they strive for. Anything short of perfection in the Navigator's mind is failure. Because of this, navigators hold themselves to a very high standard. I've heard it said that Navigators have a really hard time accepting and admitting that they were wrong (remember perfection is being free from fault). This is in fact true—Navigators hate being wrong and admitting that they're wrong.

When you have a person who is hardwired to value order, accuracy, and perfection, there are some very specific strengths that they will have. First, they will be analytical. Whether it is how they hear information or how they make decisions, Navigators will be analytical at every step of the way. Everything will be thought through. And they crave data. The more information the better. They truly believe that knowledge is power. Before making a decision, they'll give themselves time to process the information and come up with a solution that not only makes sense, but that is defendable when challenged. They're not going to go with their gut. For them, logic always trumps their emotions.

These desires will also cause them to be extremely organized. Organization is critical. Whenever I walk into a Navigator's house for the first time, there are dead giveaways to let me know exactly who they are. If they take me on a tour of the house, when we get to their bedroom closet, all of the clothes will be organized in a systematic way. Whether it's by color, by season, or whether they're separating casual clothes from office clothes from formal clothes, every item will be exactly where it belongs.

On those occasions in which we have the chance to cook together, there'll be times in which I'm looking for an item and the Navigator knows exactly where it is. I know that the minute I look into their spice cabinet, it will be the model of logical organization. Whether ordered alphabetically, or by type of cuisine, the location of every spice makes sense, and once the logic to the system is explained, the locations become easily predictable.

This organization is not just limited to their home, it applies their workspaces as well. Every paper is neatly filed, the desk is neat and orderly, and there's usually some type of inbox or to do pile where prioritized tasks can be stored until they can be properly addressed. Often there's also a calendar hanging somewhere in the cubicle as well as possibly a spreadsheet to help them stay organized with all their responsibilities. For them the mantra is, "A place for everything and everything in its place!"

Navigators are really into schedules and calendars. Having one place for all your schedules, appointments, and tasks is imperative to Navigators. If you want to talk to a Navigator, don't expect him to just be available anytime you want to drop in. Realize they want you to make an appointment because they want or need you on their calendar.

And if there's one thing Navigators love more than calendars, it's spreadsheets. Navigators love spreadsheets. Having one document that has everything on it where you can check everything out at a glance is pure gold to Navigators. Especially for Navigators with multiple projects and responsibilities, you can expect that within sight there will be a well-organized spreadsheet that they can quickly refer to, so that they can tell you at any given moment exactly what's going on.

Navigators hold themselves to very high standards. They expect the best from themselves at all times. Whether at work or at home, "good enough" is never good enough for Navigators. They also expect the same out of the people they know.

Navigators are also detail oriented. When it comes to details they are meticulous. They will often scour through every detail when others just skim through. Navigators don't have the luxury to skim. They know that the devil's in the details, and if you don't pay attention to the details, mistakes are bound to happen.

Navigators are great troubleshooters. In fact, whether it's in conversation, looking at a data analysis, or reading a business plan, the potential for trouble just seems to jump out at them. It's like they have a problem radar hard wired into their brains that catches potential issues far before they become apparent to others.

What Makes Navigators Difficult

Even with all of these great attributes, Navigators have some areas in which they need to improve. Navigators tend to be perfectionists. No, forget *tend* to be—Navigators *are* perfectionists. Everything must be perfect or they won't be satisfied. Not close to perfect, perfect: no errors, no mistakes, no nothing. Because of this, they tend to be very hard on themselves. They set high, unattainable standards for themselves, standards they'll never reach. This keeps them from being able to accept compliments, because they always feel they could've done a better job.

Unfortunately, their perfectionism isn't only focused on them, it's focused on coworkers, subordinates, friends, spouses, children, and everyone else they come into contact with. Navigators are quick to see what everyone else is doing wrong. It is difficult for them to give compliments. It's not that they're not appreciative of others' work, but why compliment someone if they haven't done a perfect job? So, they tend to be very thrifty with compliments and expressions of gratitude. But they are very generous with critiques. They not only see every little mistake, they're quick to say something about it. It's normally not a direct, "you didn't do a good job with this." That would be too assertive, and most Navigators aren't assertive. Instead, they're more likely to drop hints or communicate in some non-direct way.

I specifically remember one manager who was a Navigator who would return reports that her subordinates turned in, marked with red ink as though they were in elementary school. That's about as demotivating as it gets. And the worst part is, she thought she was helping them. In her mind, she was highlighting areas in which they could improve.

Navigators are inclined to focus on the negative. Ninety-eight percent of things can be going great, but that two percent that's wrong is killing them. They will completely ignore all the good that has been done, because they're two percent away from perfection and that two percent seems like miles to them. Not only that, but that two percent somehow was avoidable in their mind and they can't figure out how they missed it, or why they trusted someone else to do it. It is hard for them to be satisfied (I know, some will say that not being satisfied is a good thing), but this is beyond a dissatisfaction that drives someone to do better. It's hard for Navigators to be happy.

This negativity also shows up as pessimism when new ideas are presented to them. They will quickly say things like, "Let me tell you why that won't work." I'm not talking about an attempt to come up with a better solution or to fix a problem. I'm talking about inserting negativity into a situation, but doing so with the illusion of being helpful. Other times they'll use the phrase, "I'm just playing the devil's advocate," as a way of justifying their intentions. I'm not saying that you shouldn't correct others nor am I saying that this phrase is taboo, but if you have a constant need to tell people why their ideas are bad, maybe the ideas aren't the problem.

Navigator's desire for perfection along with the fact they often internalize their mistakes makes it very difficult for them to admit mistakes and apologize. Rarely will the Navigator just say, "I'm sorry." Instead, there is usually some long explanation of what happened, and it often involves either the mistakes of someone else, or something completely beyond their control. And if a mistake is actually made, don't expect to hear, "I'm sorry!" Normally you'll just hear "Oh." Or they'll just keep moving as though nothing happened.

Navigator's pursuit of perfection makes them slow to make decisions. They spend great amounts of time gathering as much information as possible so they can be certain that their decision is right. But the certainty they seek is rarely attainable, so even after collecting as much data as possible, they're often still stuck agonizing over the uncomfortable reality that they're about to make a decision without absolute certainty. So they'll wait, making everyone who is depending on their input wait as well. This causes great harm to the team's productivity as the Navigator works from paralysis of analysis.

Although Navigators rarely give compliments, as it turns out, they need to receive a lot of them. More than the other types, Navigators tend to internalize their mistakes. For them, it's very hard to separate making a wrong decision with being wrong. They tend to replay their mistakes over and over again, beating themselves up over what is now clear through 20/20 vision. That coupled with receiving criticism can be enough to put Navigators into depression. Navigators need positive feedback and encouragement. It's one of the few things that counteract the effect of that inner critic between their ears, that voice that rings in their head nonstop telling them that they and what they are doing are not good enough.

Most Navigators prefer to be alone or with small groups of people. Alone time allows them time to process. Plus, for most Navigators, a large amount of social interaction, regardless of how good they are at it, can be draining. When it comes to work, they'd rather get things done themselves than rely on working in teams. Teams can be draining, inefficient, and unreliable. That doesn't mean they're not a team player, but let's be honest, who else is going to be able to get things done the way they want them done?

How to Work with Navigators

When working with Navigators, the first key is to be detailed in your communication. Whether it's job expectations, updates on a project, or the mission of the organization, Navigators need clear, detailed communication at all times. They don't just want to know the what and the when; they want to know the why, the how, and the who as well. A clear understanding is needed before they will begin working. Remember, they're charting a course and figuring out a pathway to make your plans a reality. They will use all of the information at their disposal to chart the best course possible. But with this information, there can be no room for error and especially no room for ambiguity.

Be patient in providing explanations. Don't be offended if they ask a lot of questions. The need for accurate detailed information is critical, and they want to fill in any potential gaps or misunderstandings before any work begins. Asking the questions allows them to focus on the tasks. And some of the questions may reveal potential problems that they want you to see before they happen.

Allow Navigators to become subject matter experts and recognize them for it. Most Navigators enjoy working with the details, and they're good at it. Let them be the go-to people for expertise in those areas. This also allows them to be recognized for their vast knowledge.

Never, never, never over promise. Once you make a commitment to a Navigator, they're going to hold you to it. Make sure that you only commit to what you are sure will happen. No best-case scenarios. It's better to give a conservative estimate than to over promise and lose all credibility.

Plus, in general, Navigators are more comfortable with the possibility of incremental improvements than they are with exponential improvements. Incremental improvements seem more attainable and reasonable. It's not a detriment to give Navigators a conservative estimate, it's to your benefit.

And for the love of all that is good, before letting Navigators give presentations to a group, make sure they've been thoroughly trained and coached. This is not a statement of a Navigator's ability to communicate; it's about how they process information and thus how they expect others to do the same. Navigators focus primarily on details and data, it's what connects with them. It's what moves them. In fact, they often believe that all the other things that make up a presentation, things like presentation style, humor, etc., are unnecessary. The problem is that they, like everyone else, believe that what moves them moves everyone. This will lead to long, drawn out, monotone presentations. They give information without regard for how it's presented or how well the audience will comprehend the information. And in the end, no one will be certain of what they're supposed to do.

Remember, Navigators pride themselves on being accurate and detail-oriented. Organization is key for them as they prefer to work with structured systems. They're analytical and are fact finders. They want their work to be detailed and precise. They're conscientious, careful, and have high standards of quality.

Ways to Make Deposits with Navigators

Consistent Communication/Effective Communication

Using the various communication vehicles available to convey information on a regular basis.

Predictability/Consistency

Exhibiting the same behavior and responses to similar situations.

Clearly defined expectations

Stating verbally and in written form what you expect the organization, teams, and individuals to achieve. Expectations should be Specific, Measurable, Attainable, Realistic, and given a Timeframe (SMART).

Accurate information

Sharing data or communicating information that has been confirmed as being factual.

Ways to Make Withdrawals with Navigators

Giving responsibility without authority/Not providing proper resources

Giving a duty or assignment without making for which a person will be held accountable without providing either the authority or means needed for success.

Flexibility

Allowing individuals the freedom to find their own unique ways to accomplish tasks and solve problems when appropriate.

Not giving enough information

Communicating inconsistently and without providing adequate details.

Chapter 11

A FEW ADDITIONAL COMMENTS ON PERSONALITIES

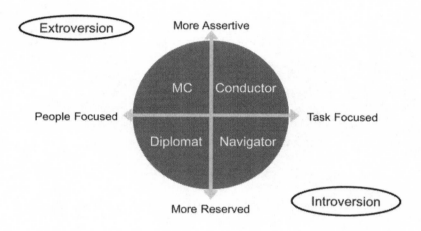

You'll notice the personality diagram has vertical and horizontal arrows. In many ways, the diagram is set up to be like a graph and the arrows serve as axes. Where the arrows intersect is the zero point of the graph. The stronger your personality, in any category, the farther you move from the center.

As you follow the horizontal arrow to the right you have personalities with work styles that are more performance or task focused. These personalities will be more motivated by getting things done, even during conflict, their conflict resolution styles will be more focused on who was right.

As you move in the opposite direction along the horizontal axis, the left, those personality styles are more people focused. Goals and productivity don't motivate them the way that people and their well-being do.

As you move up the vertical axis, you increase in assertiveness. Assertiveness is primarily relational and can be viewed as a communication style. People who are more assertive are more outspoken; they're quick to speak out and make their opinions and feelings known. They are more forceful. They are more likely to try and take control of a situation or influence others. In general, they exude more energy, move at a faster pace, and make decisions more quickly.

As you move down the vertical axis, you decrease in assertiveness and become more reserved. Being reserved is not a bad thing; it's just a style of communication and of relating to people. People who are more reserved are less likely to speak out and make their opinions known in the direct way. They are far subtler and nuanced in their conversation. They move at a slower pace and are often slower to address problems or make decisions.

As you move diagonally down between the axis towards the bottom right of the diagram, towards the Navigator, you increase in introversion. As you move directly up to the left towards the MC, you increase in extroversion. Introversion and extroversion are often misunderstood. Being extroverted is not a measure of how dynamic and boisterous a person is. Nor is being extroverted a measure of shyness or being quiet. Extroversion and introversion are measures of how energy flows during human interaction. If spending time with other people energizes you, then you are extroverted. If spending time with other people is draining to you, then you are introverted. I know plenty of introverted people who are very social and very personable. But after interacting with people, they often need a break. They need to recharge. And although most extroverts are rather social and boisterous, I do you know some extroverts who come across as shy and subdued. But they require social interaction; it energizes them and allows them to move forward.

Where this really becomes important at work is that for people who are extroverted if their work causes them to be isolated, they will often take breaks to go and find social interaction. This could be the cause of a lot of frustration to the other people who work with them, as it may interrupt their work. Conversely, when people who are introverted have jobs that cause them to interact with people constantly, they may need some alone time to get revitalized. That doesn't mean that they can't do a great job at it, they just need some sanity breaks.

In general, personality types are descriptions of who people are in their natural state. People change and adapt over time. They add and subtract different behaviors into their toolbox, mostly based on their experiences and their needs.

Now that you've been introduced to the four personality types, there are a few things that need to be said. First, each person has at least one personality type. Some only have one, but most are a blend of types. Many who have a blend of types have a dominant type, one that is heads and shoulders above the rest.

This means that very few people have all of the strengths and weaknesses of any one personality type. There are some that will be more prevalent than others. But just like they have blended personalities, they'll have blended strengths and weaknesses. Also, the strength and weaknesses won't be equally distributed either. Some people may have a majority of strengths of one type, but their weaknesses fall into another category.

Personality blends are usually combinations of things that are adjacent to another on the chart. For example, on the diagram, Conductors combine with Navigators or they may combine with MCs. MCs combine with Navigators and Diplomats. Diplomats combine with MCs and Navigators. Navigators combine with Diplomats and MCs. It is seldom that personalities that are diagonal from one another combine. Although it does happen, it is rare. Often there is something else going on.

For many, there are times where they keep their personality restrained. They try to be themselves, but they know that they have thoughts and behaviors that won't be accepted by others or are not beneficial in a situation. Sometimes it's done consciously, like when a person's job responsibilities demand behaviors that are different than their natural behaviors. For example, if you have an MC who is given a role that requires a great attention to detail, like being a payroll manager. Over time, he may begin to focus more on details and organization because he has to. He may even begin to value these attributes. He has to in order to succeed or even survive in his new role. But his core needs—attention and praise—don't change. He's not a Navigator, he's simply an MC wearing a Navigator mask.

Masks are more common than we'd like to believe. Sometimes, they happen unconsciously, almost naturally. We adapt to circumstances, expectations, or other strong personalities without realizing that we're doing it. I have seen many Conductors who appear to be diplomats when in the presence of their Conductor boss. Other times, there is a conscious decision to adapt behaviors to be accepted. Three of the most common sources of masks are influence from parents, job positions that call for skills different than those of your personality, and the military.

For example, let's say you have someone who is a Diplomat, a person who really values peace and stability. But what if, growing up, she had parents who were always pushing her to be something other than who she was? What if she was being told over and over again "to be great, you need to be more aggressive. You need to grab life by the horns and take control," and so on. It's likely that she would begin taking on behaviors more reminiscent of a Conductor. She would be far more ambitious. She would become more assertive or possibly even aggressive. She would pursue control and leadership. She would become more independent. But she wouldn't become a Conductor. Although her behaviors would be that of a Conductor, she will still have the same basic Diplomat needs: peace, trust, and self-worth, but her behaviors would be misleading. She is a Diplomat wearing a Conductor mask.

It can be difficult to tell when someone is wearing a mask. Without someone actually taking a detailed assessment, the only thing you initially have to go on is their behaviors. And at times that can be misleading. As you get to know the person, you'll begin to notice that although they have certain behaviors, there is something just not right about it. Sometimes it's that it seems forced or insincere. At other times, you'll notice they need a break from those behaviors. Periodically, you'll notice that when they get what should meet their need, they still function more in their weakness than in their strength. All of those are indicators that they may be wearing a mask.

Wearing a mask can be draining. Pretending to be someone you're not, especially for long periods of time, can be taxing even when you're not fully aware that you're doing it. Minor adaptations for limited periods of time can be relatively easy to deal with, but wearing a mask can cause stress—the type of stress that can affect your mental well-being as well as your overall health. Coming to grips with who you really are and accepting yourself as you are for many is a life-changing (and sometimes life-saving) event.

Chapter 12

BLIND SPOTS—BE A FORCE MULTIPLIER, NOT A FORCE DIVIDER!

Being a force multiplier should be the goal of everyone in leadership, and truthfully, every leader is capable of becoming a force multiplier. But in all honesty a lot of "leaders" spend more time disrupting work than they do multiplying it. They feel a need to "stay on top of things" in an unhealthy way, so they call unnecessary meetings, they micromanage, they randomly show up at people's desks interrupting whatever they're working on to redirect their focus on something else, they fail to give pertinent information, they play favorites, they fail to recognize individual's contributions to the team, and, when frustrated or overwhelmed, they pass their anxiety down to the people they lead. All of these things actually disrupt work.

Others don't see their blind spots. Even though there are things they do that are great, for most there are things they do that hinder their leadership as well. The problem is that often people aren't even aware of it. As a leader, it's easy to look at others and see what they do that makes them difficult, but one challenge that we all face is our own blind spots, the things that make us difficult that sometimes we're not even aware of.

That's what this chapter is all about. Each personality has its blind spots, the things that keep us from being force multipliers.

The more we can neutralize them, the more effective a leader we'll be. So, let's have a conversation, just you and me.

Suggestions for Conductors

Don't Talk Down to Others

If you're a Conductor, you likely have a tendency to talk down to others. It's normally a combination of directness and impatience and often not only are you not aware of what you're doing it, it is unintentional. It's easy to get impatient, especially when you feel that people aren't moving fast enough. It's even more difficult when you feel that you have to keep explaining things. I know you hate to explain things especially when you have to do it over and over, but you can't let that be an excuse for disrespecting people. You know how you hate to be disrespected. And let's be honest, sometimes you know you're doing it, but you're justifying it. Be patient. You have no idea the damage you're doing when this happens. Every time it happens, you're disengaging your team.

And whatever you do, don't let your anger get the best of you. When you're ticked off, don't say what you're feeling, no matter how good you think it will make you feel. Go somewhere and cool off. Get your head together. It's not worth the damage you'll do. Ambrose Bierce once said, "Speak when you are angry and you will make the best speech you will ever regret."

Don't Abuse Your Authority; Earn Respect

As important as respect is, the best type is earned. I'm saying this because it's easy when you get into a position of authority to let the power go to your head. To feel like, now people need to respect you. Don't abuse it. Don't become some tyrant running around the office instilling fear in everyone because you now got your shot.

By the way, don't think that if they fear you, that means they respect you. Those are two very different things. There is a huge difference between fear and respect. Fear is just invoking a negative emotion in other people; it's having them view you as a threat. Yeah, they may do what you tell them, but they're not respecting you. They also won't work hard for you, they won't take ownership of the project, and they certainly won't be loyal to you. They'll comply, but you'll never get the best out of them.

Respect happens when people think highly of you. You are viewed with and given honor. It's different than someone liking you; in fact, you can respect someone especially for their character or work and still not like them as a person. Respect is earned. It can be earned by doing what's right. It can be earned by having integrity especially when it's easy to compromise your integrity. It can be earned by working hard and doing your best. It can be earned by standing up for yourself or for others. It can be earned by showing respect for others.

Earn it! If you do, you'll have a team or a relationship that is not only productive, but loyal. If you don't, it's not you they're respecting; they're respecting the seat you sit in. And when you're gone and you no longer have that seat, you'll also no longer have their respect. And I guarantee that if it's fear you have, you don't want to know what they're saying behind your back.

Practice Delegation; Be a Team Player

Be a team player. A team player is simply a person who works well as a member of a team or group. That means you don't always have to be the leader. Be a good follower when that's your role. Play your position. Don't disrupt the team dynamic because you don't like how things are going or you want them to go faster. Consider how your actions may affect the entire group. That means if you're in a meeting, don't act like you don't want to be there because you already know all the stuff they're talking about; stay engaged. Don't do things to undermine others; play nice. Don't withhold information from others; share.

As a leader, delegate (more on how to do that later.) I know that you hate giving up control, but you have to let go and let people do their jobs. And just because someone messed up once doesn't mean you need to keep them in the doghouse. Nor does it mean that everyone's going to mess up so they can't be trusted. Distribute your work so you can focus on what's important. The more you complain about how much you have to do, the more of an indictment it is on your lack of delegation.

Make a Personal Connection with Workers

People need social activity at work. More important, they need to feel connected, especially to their supervisor. Without that connection, your team will never be as committed, loyal, or productive as they could be. Even though you may feel you don't need that "soft stuff" to be effective, it's not about you. Your job is to free people up to be the best employee they can be. So, go make some deposits.

Be Aware of How You Project Yourself to Others (Smile)

Most people are completely unaware of their default facial expression. Conductors tend to be even less aware and often less concerned. Many Conductors' default expression looks like a frown or scowl (I don't know why, but this one's pretty consistent; it's also the case for Navigators). You take that expression, combine it with very assertive and direct communication, and the occasional talking down to people and you have a recipe for disaster.

When my youngest son was three years old, I walked past his room and saw him in the mirror practicing his cry. As he stood directly in front of the mirror, he would cry for a moment then observe his face from different angles to make sure it was convincing enough. Clearly, he had determined that if he mastered crying, he had a better chance of getting what he wanted. If my son at three was smart enough to know how to appeal to someone's emotions to be more effective, what about you?

I'm not saying be fake or manipulative, but realize that people are judging your emotions and intent while interpreting your words through the facial expression you display. And they see those expressions often before they hear your words. If they see your expression and words are in conflict, most people are going to go with what they see over what they hear. Am I saying walk around smiling all day like you're on drugs? No! But I am saying, be aware of how you come across to people. It makes a huge difference.

Common Withdrawals Conductors Make

Not listening

Physically not paying attention when people are speaking; showing annoyance or indifference about what people are saying.

Bursts of anger/Fits of rage

Inability to control emotional responses during stressful situations or when angry; using profanity, yelling, pounding on furniture, and slamming doors are examples of bursts of anger.

Usurping authority

Showing disregard for established authority through open criticism or secretly doing things that go against the authority.

Suggestions for MCs

Provide Succinct Communication (not stories, tangents, or gossip)

If there's one thing MCs have a reputation for, it's talking. Unfortunately, that reputation is not positive. You have a talent. Your communication skills are a gift. But when you're not in control of that gift, it becomes a curse.

You don't always need to tell stories. There really are times when you can just get to the point. Sometimes just say what needs to be said and that's all. This will be helpful to everyone and will improve your reputation. Don't be the person everyone avoids when they see coming, because they don't want to be tied up for long periods of time with endless stories.

Which reminds me, make sure to respect other people's time. It's good to have some chat time, but make sure you're focusing on work while you're at work. If people are in the middle of something important, come back unless what you have to say is urgent. And don't wait until they're ready to leave work to start a conversation. Seriously, don't do that.

The one exception to all of this is when giving directions or updates on projects to Diplomats or Navigators. Be willing to give details. I know you feel that you've given enough information, but they need details, especially if they need them to get something done. And don't get frustrated when you're asked questions. It's not a personal attack (even though it may feel that way). They are trying to get the information they need to complete the task. Give them the information, and do it without coming across as bothered or irritated.

Also, don't gossip. Don't participate in it at all. I know that's hard because you get some juicy stuff coming your way, but the moment you start gossiping, you're losing respect. Eventually the people you're gossiping to will wonder what you say about them behind their backs. Let it go, don't do it.

This also means, when you're dealing with a problem at work, especially a conflict, don't just go with the first story you hear. There's an old proverb that says, "The first to present his case seems right until another comes and questions him." You may be completely convinced of what happened based on the first version you hear, but remember it's only one side of the story. Get both sides, and then deal with it.

Practice Time Management and Organizational Skills; End Procrastination

It's time to stop being late, to stop missing assignments, and to stop forgetting appointments. Write things down! Get some type of organizer, and use it! You don't have to use every piece of it and become its slave. But you need to have something where you can immediately record any commitments into a calendar with reminders. Make sure to use those reminders; you don't want to wait and be reminded when it's due. This will also help keep you from double booking appointments.

You should have a basic to-do list for the day. It doesn't have to be complex, but you need a basic plan. You will still have the freedom to wing it within your day, but don't sacrifice important items for your freedom.

This also applies to how you lead your team. You need to keep a record of people's responsibilities so that you can hold them accountable. This will also help you keep track of projects and things you've delegated. This may seem complicated, but let me give you a simple solution. Ask a Navigator for help getting organized. Don't feel ashamed or feel that it would have them see you in a lesser light. They already see it, trust me they do. Ask them for help. They'll be glad to do it and it will help strengthen your relationship. You'll make a deposit.

Don't Over-Promise

It happens all the time. You get caught off guard. You're not looking at your calendar (because certainly you've heeded my last "suggestion"). And in the moment, you make a commitment that if you'd had time to think about, there's no way you would have agreed to it.

Don't be rash with your commitments. Take a moment and ask yourself: "Do I have time to do this? What is involved? What other commitments do I already have?" You have to learn to say "no" or at least "let me look at my schedule and get back to you." I know you don't like to say no and let people down. Trust me, saying yes and not delivering is far worse. You talk about a huge withdrawal.

And I know that there are times when you commit to doing something and you not only fail to do it, you forget that you ever said it. Write it down!

Have a Plan and Don't Constantly Change the Plan

I know you love to improvise; it gives you freedom to create, but when you're leading other people you cannot subject them to that type of chaos. Even though you don't need one, other people need a clear plan. They need to understand what is to be accomplished, how it's going to be done, and what their roles are. That doesn't happen without a plan that's clearly communicated. Give them what they need to help make your goal a success.

Also, I know you're talented, but be careful about not having a plan when you give presentations or lead meetings. You're probably skilled enough to just go up there and do your thing, but there are a few problems. First, when you wing it, you're more likely to go over your time. That's not good. It may not bother you, but it's disrespectful to everyone that comes after you, the person who planned the meeting (assuming you didn't plan it), and the audience members.

Second, when you wing it, you're not prepared (I know that was given to you from the redundancy department.) This means that your facts aren't always going to be accurate. That's a problem. It could be a major problem if people take action based on those "facts," and it could be an embarrassing problem if someone calls you out on it.

Filter Your Words

I know that there are a lot of times where you're in the middle of a conversation and the funniest, sarcastic little comment pops into your mind, sometimes it's the perfect comeback, to what someone else said. But here's the problem—your brain works way faster than your filter. Your personality type is more likely than any other to say something inappropriate or hurtful while trying to be funny. Think before you speak. Without knowing it, you could be making withdrawals. Years ago, we were putting together a facilitator's manual for small group discussions and one of my colleagues came up with the best line: "Don't say something stupid, like the first thing that comes into your mind."

Common Withdrawals for MCs

Stealing credit

Attributing success or achievement to one's self instead of acknowledging everyone who contributed; out-right taking credit for something that belongs to someone else.

Gossip

Sharing details about private discussions or sensitive information about others without their permission.

Not giving enough information

Communicating inconsistently and without providing adequate details.

Suggestions for Diplomats

Learn to Confront Problems (face to face)

For you Diplomats, peace is critical, I know. So, one of your biggest challenges is going to come when your peace is either at risk or has been completely annihilated. When conflict rears its ugly head, you can't run from it. First of all, it's part of your job so you have to deal with it. Second, not all conflict is bad (what is bad is the build-up that occurs when people avoid necessary conflict). It's critical to not avoid the conflict that is disrupting your peace, especially if you're a leader.

Here's the deal. Ignoring it is not going to make it go away. You need to nip it in the bud while it's still small. When it's small, it's easier to deal with. Don't give it a chance to grow.

Even if the conflict has already erupted, you still have to deal with it. Bring the two parties together in private and work it out. It's not the huge monster you've made it out to be in your mind. You can do this!

And, make sure you deal with it face to face. No emails, not texting, face to face. I know it feels less threatening to not have to see people's face when you address it, but when you deal with conflict via text or email, you invite miscommunication. There is no tone or non-verbal communication to go along with the words. You have no idea how your words will be interpreted. But you can be sure that they'll be taken wrong. You're just going to make it worse. Trust me on this one.

Also, whatever you do, don't deal with it in a meeting. This is actually one of my pet peeves because I've seen how destructive it can be. If it's a one- or two-person issue, don't make it a team issue. First, the people who aren't involved in it at all will either believe it's about them or will become affected by the situation. Second, those who are involved either won't think it's about them or will be too embarrassed to focus on the issue. They'll just get defensive.

Avoid Sentimentality

Empathy is one of your greatest strengths, but it's not the only tool in your tool chest. You have to fight the urge to be sentimental when something else, like discipline or tough love, would be more appropriate. There are times when people are just wrong and they need to be called on it. There are times when people are unreliable and need to be held accountable. And there are times when people make excuses, and you're not doing them a favor if you let them excuse themselves from their responsibilities.

Sometimes as a leader the best thing for a person is not the thing they want, it's the thing they need. Be willing to truly help them be the best contributor they can be. The funny thing is, you usually know when you're being sentimental. You're not getting caught off guard; you can feel it. Don't let sentimentality be your weakness and don't become an enabler for people to not be their best.

Practice Risk Taking

There's no way around it; you have to take risks. Not everything has to be a risk, but there are times when the status quo must be disrupted. Often, it's in the form of change, and you can't deny it. Take a chance on someone that you believe in, but never got a shot. Take a chance on a technology that you know will be beneficial to your team or your organization. Take a chance on change. Learn to find comfort in discomfort.

Avoid Being Critical and Judgmental; Don't Negative Bond

In saying that, make sure you're not an obstacle to change either. It's easy when things are uncomfortable to resist change. But you have even a greater temptation. You've built so many relationships with people and they not only trust you, they're emotionally bonded to you. You can't go around expressing your displeasure. You have to be careful not to cause a rebellion regardless of whether or not that's your intent.

If you start sharing your concerns about a change or risk with other people, because they're genuinely concerned about you, they may turn their empathy into feeling the same way about things as you do. Negativity is contagious. And people often bond over things they both disagree with. In fact, negativity can pull a neutral person to the dark side. I call this negative bonding. Here's a common example for you:

Let's say you're at the grocery store. You go to check out, and there are 30 to 40 people waiting, but only four checkout lanes. You think to yourself, "You know, I'm having a good day, and I'm not in a rush to go anywhere, so no big deal." But in front of you there's a person who is clearly agitated by the whole thing who keeps tapping their feet and looking around impatiently. Finally, they turn to you and say, "This is ridiculous! I can't believe this! Can you?"

What are they trying to do? They're trying to pull you into their bad day. At this moment, you have to be careful not to let your empathy get in the way. In this moment, you have two choices. You can choose to agree with them and make yourself vulnerable to their negativity. Or you can defuse the situation; perhaps by saying something like, "I'm sure the cashiers are overwhelmed by all of this as well."

It's easy to do, and honestly it feels kinda good in the moment to have people there with you. But you must make sure you're not being that person. Don't be the source of negative bonding.

Make Important Decisions in a Timely Manner

One of your many strengths is that you work very well in a team environment. In fact, while leading a team you are naturally inclined to promote collaboration. You keep people involved. You help the group come to consensus and that's a great attribute.

But there are times when collaborative decision making isn't practical. The group won't always come to a consensus. Sometimes it can take too long. There are times you have to be willing to make decisions for the group. That is part of your job responsibility.

And it doesn't just happen in meetings. There are rarely times when everyone is going to be thrilled with your decision. But you still have to make them. Don't delay decisions worrying about how it will affect everyone. Make the best decision you can and go with it. We're all big boys and girls. We can handle it.

Common Withdrawals Diplomats Make

Unresolved Issues

Failing to address both performance and behavioral issues.

Passive/Aggressive

Indirectly resisting to avoid conflict; examples include procrastination, sabotage, and phrasing an objection in a sarcastic or rhetorical manner.

Keeping People in the Doghouse

Refusing to forgive a mistake; consistently reminding the offender and others of the mistake; and refusing to give the offender a chance to do anything else for fear that they will make the same mistake.

Suggestions for Navigators

Embrace Change

In a previous chapter, we discussed thinking outside of the box. Even though some Navigators are extremely creative, the truth is the proverbial "box" was built primarily by Navigators. The box represents consistency and quality. It allows for repeatable processes. In the box is safety and comfort. But here's the warning. Don't fall in love with the box.

Boxes, as great as they are, are only temporary. At some point they all become obsolete, and usually Navigators are the last to acknowledge it because they want the consistency that the box brings.

You have to accept change. You have to not only accept it, you have to embrace it. Yeah, I know it's uncomfortable. I know there are a lot of unknowns. But it's necessary. There's only two choices in business: adapt or die. The beautiful thing is after the change has been figured out, you can build another box for the new change. You can make it work better and more consistently. But stop fighting change.

Improve Communication Style

Here's something ironic. Even though MCs get on your nerves, the two of you have a big thing in common. You both like to talk. I know you think you don't, but you do. The difference is that where the MC likes to talk about themselves and tell stories, you like to talk about the details. All of the details. Trust me there are times where all of the details are important. But not all of the time.

There are actually times when getting to the point is not only sufficient, it is preferred. Too many details can cloud the very point you're trying to make. Directions get lost in the details. Action items get lost in the details. What people need to take away from the conversation gets lost in the details. The ability to give the right amount of information can be critical not only to your ability to clearly communicate your message. It can have dramatic effects on you career path as well. This is especially true when talking to Conductors and MCs

I know you're probably thinking, "If I just give them the bottom line, then they're going to ask for the details anyway. So, I might as well give them to them up front." No, they won't, trust me. They may ask for a few clarifications, but they don't have time or desire to hear all of the details. They're ready to move on to something else.

What's interesting is that as people climb higher up the organizational chart, their roles go from being production oriented to being strategic. In that world, at any given time, people are juggling multiple responsibilities and undertakings. They have to get things done quickly, and they need information in small bite size quantities, so they can move to the next item. How you communicate with them will make you either a valued asset or an inconvenience to be avoided.

Delegate

Similar to what I said to the Conductors, you must be willing to delegate. But your situation's different. Where Conductors don't like to delegate because they don't want to lose control, your issue is related to being a perfectionist. I get it. You can do it better than anyone else, but is that always what's best?

The question you have to ask is what's the best use of your time? Your expertise should be utilized in the areas that benefit the organization the most. The other things, although important, become training and development opportunities. But you have to let go and let someone else do it.

Be an Encouragement

As a leader, it's important that corrective feedback isn't the only type of feedback you give. Employees need to know not only what they need to improve, but they need to be commended when they do a good job. This will have tremendous effects not only on loyalty and retention but on productivity as well.

Unfortunately, if you're slanted toward being a perfectionist, you'll have to make a special effort to make commendations.

Make Decisions in a Timely Manner

It's important for you to make decisions in a timely manner. I know that you want to wait until everything is unquestionably certain. That is the optimal situation; unfortunately the optional situation rarely exists.

There are many times when speed trumps quality. There's a saying that "the difference between salad and garbage is timing." This can also be true of decisions. A perfect decision made too late is garbage.

And the truth is, you pretty much know what the answer is anyway. Even though you want to go back and double and triple check it, you already know the answer. So, when time is of the essence, make the decision and move on. If it doesn't turn out perfect, don't take it personally. It's not a reflection of who you are; it's a reflection of the circumstances around you.

This also includes those moments when there is no plan. I know, you're not an improviser. But, you can't always wait for a plan to start moving. Sometimes the plan becomes apparent after you start. Sure, it's not the ideal situation, but waiting for the plan to appear can be disastrous to everyone.

Common Withdrawals Navigators Make

Failing to give recognition

Omitting praise when people achieve something; failing to plan celebrations for major accomplishments or special life events.

Constant criticism and destructive comments

Tendency to make negative statements about people's performance or character. This is particularly harmful when done publicly or as a form of humor.

Adding your two cents

Providing unsolicited opinion in a rude manner. Constantly trying to prove how smart you are.

Chapter 13

SEVEN KEYS TO BEING
A FORCE MULTIPLIER

Now that we've covered our blind spots, let's talk about seven things that every leader should do to increase their force multiplication.

1. Treat everyone with dignity and respect.

This is the most fundamental rule for being an effective leader, as well as a decent human being. Unfortunately, it's also one of the most violated. The way we treat people says a lot about who we are. As a leader, it also determines your long-term effectiveness.

How does this happen to decent human beings? For that we'll need a little history on the subject of Scientific Management:

> In the mid 1950's, Douglas McGregor, a professor at the MIT School of Industrial Management, began teaching a management theory that would challenge the conventional view of management and leave an indelible mark on businesses around the world. In his book *The Human Side of Enterprise* (McGraw-Hill, 1960,) he unveiled to the world the idea of Theory X and Theory Y. It encapsulated a fundamental distinction between management styles and has formed the basis for much subsequent writing on the subject.

142

In short, Theory X assumed that employees are naturally unmotivated, dislike working, have little to no ambition, and in general will do the least amount of work they can get away with. This encouraged the leader to take a more "hands on," "authoritarian" style of leadership because workers need to be supervised at every step or work would slow to a halt.

In contrast, Theory Y assumed that most people in the workforce actually want to do their job and do it well under the right conditions. It supposed that people seek and accept responsibility and in fact will perform better with greater responsibility. This encouraged leadership to provide more opportunities to realize one's' potential and talents. This leads to a more decentralized leadership structure with greater delegation.

What is often missed in McGregor's theory is that he wasn't introducing two new revolutionary management theories. In fact, Theory X not only wasn't new, it was the status quo across most industries in the United States. Theory X was the natural result of the implementation of Scientific Management and McGregor was attempting to undo its effects.

In 1911, Frederick Taylor published *The Principles of Scientific Management* (Harper & Brothers Publishers, 1911), a compilation of his theories on Scientific Management. Scientific Management was the product of Taylor's pursuit of economic efficiency. Initially introduced as "Shop Management," Scientific Management rejected the popular belief that the work performed in the industrial labor force could not be effectively analyzed and optimized. He set out to investigate how work was performed, and then scrutinized every aspect of that job (what percentage of time should be allowed to rest) with the aim of optimizing worker productivity.

The results of Taylor's work produced many benefits that are still observable in today's workforce. He developed what would later be known as standard operating procedures, a consistent method of performing a job or work function, replacing the old and often unreliable rule of thumb. He also pioneered the idea of managers having different work responsibilities than workers.

Many of Taylor's findings, including the fact that a certain number of breaks (or a certain percentage of time at rest) is necessary for maximum productivity, were very positive and are still appreciated today. But one of the unfortunate impacts of Taylor's work came not from his scientific discoveries, but from his own personal biases. Taylor viewed laborers and workers as "stupid and phlegmatic," whereas he viewed managers as educated and intelligent, referring to them as men of necessity. Whether intended or not, this type of thinking came with many natural by-products, which among others include: The belief that workers are lazy and will do the least amount of work possible, have no ambition, and are primarily motivated by money. Thus, management's primary role must be to counteract an inherent human tendency to avoid work.

Eventually, this type of thinking created a type of caste system in which those in management positions believed they were superior to those who they believe aren't smart enough or talented enough to join the management ranks.

In many organizations, this leadership hierarchy still exists. Many in leadership positions assume they're actually better than those they lead. Better workers, better assets to the organization, and in many cases, better people. And when people think they're better than others, it becomes easier to justify treating them poorly. This manifests itself in rudeness, disrespect, and other things far worse.

Unfortunately, rudeness and disrespect have run rampant in our society and its effects are seen all over the workplace. Whether bullying, threatening, humiliating, or intimidating, or blatant acts of disrespect, many leaders have become infected with the disease of disrespect. Certain acts are easy to spot. They yell, they threaten either with physical violence or some form of career retaliation, they call people derogatory names, and it's often intentional. Sometimes it's purely out of anger. Other times, it's some warped view of a management tool. A leader sees a coach yelling at his players or a drill sergeant in the face of new recruits, and they walk away with the misguided impression that disrespect is not only appropriate, but effective.

But not all disrespect is that overt. It's also the small actions taken throughout the day, especially when you're in a bad mood or worse, have a bad history with someone. They don't receive the benefit of the doubt. They're viewed as sources of frustration. They receive less patience. And they feel every instance of it. The little acts of rudeness that occur over and over again may not seem significant, but they act as a form of Lingchi, death by a thousand cuts. And the results are a bitter, frustrated, and demotivated workforce.

How you view people determines how you treat them, and how you treat them often determines their behavior. When people are treated as though they are unmotivated or unreliable, our actions communicate our true feelings. Regardless of what we say, they experience our true intent. Ralph Waldo Emerson's quote, "What you do speaks so loudly, I can't hear what you are saying," comes to mind.

Many leaders inherit people who've already been demotivated by their previous manager. One of the challenges I often give to new leaders is to treat everyone you lead with dignity and respect, regardless of how they treat you, for 30 days. There's a reason it takes 30 days, especially for new leaders. What they don't realize is for the first 3-9 months, their direct reports aren't treating them based on who they are and what they do. No, they are being treated based on who the previous leader was. And if the previous leader was a jerk, guess what you've inherited. It takes time for you to undo their previous experience through consistent behavior.

Although some don't take the challenges, the ones that do are often stunned by the results. People who have been consistently difficult to lead become more responsive and people with attitudes become more a part of the team. And productivity increases.

2. Be fair and unbiased

One dangerous dynamic that occurs in many workplaces is playing favorites. People sense when there is favoritism and whether it is based on a dimension of diversity (race, gender, ability, religion, etc.) or relationships, it damages those who are not the favorites.

But, treating everyone fairly is far easier said than done. The truth is we all have people we naturally get along with. We may share something in common, whether it's NASCAR, politics, or romantic comedies, we like to be around people who share our same interests. And some are just easier to get along with in general.

At the same time, we all have people that naturally get on our last nerve. The people that if no one were looking we would smother them with a pillow and hide their body. Okay, that may have been a little extreme, but you get me. There are people that just rub us the wrong way, yet we have to see them every day.

The challenge is to treat both categories of people and everyone in between equally. Equally isn't quite the right word; there will be some distinctions because some will merit more time, attention, and praise based on their performance. But we do need to treat them based on how they are as employees, not how they make us feel.

The problem is that if we don't intentionally make the effort, we naturally play favorites. People that are easier to get along with we treat better. And people who flatter us and inflate our ego receive special treatment. Some would claim to be immune to flattery; the question is would their direct reports agree?

3. Have a positive, enthusiastic attitude every day (and spread it to your employees)

So, we've all been there. We have something important to tell our supervisor, it can't wait. As we get closer to her office, we see the look on her face. We can see her mood and we quickly decide, "It can wait."

Attitude is everything. And to a leader it is a tool that can completely change the environment of a team. Colin Powell has been famously quoted as saying, "Perpetual Optimism is a Force Multiplier."

We all know that person who is always up, always optimistic. They always have something positive to say. When they hear bad news, they just smile, laugh, and move on. Nothing seems to bother them.

When those people don't get on our nerves, they have an amazing impact on us. Just their smile can have an impact on us.

In a Swedish study[1] by Marianne Sonnby–Borgström, subjects were shown pictures of people displaying various emotions. When the subject was shown a picture of someone smiling, they were asked to frown. Amazingly, they found that instead of a frown, the facial expressions went directly to reproducing what they saw. It actually took conscious effort for the subjects to frown. The power of smile or a good attitude is far more powerful than most are aware.

Unfortunately, we also know negative people. The people who never have anything positive to say. The ones who feel it's their job to "bring everyone back to reality" when things are going too well. The ones who shoot down every idea. The one's whose favorite phrases are, "Here's why that won't work," and "I'm just playing devil's advocate."

Leaders who are negative are not innovators nor do they lead innovative teams. They miss out on opportunities to be innovative. When opportunity comes, they don't believe it. They shoot it down because they always have a reason why things either can't work or can't be done. Over time, their direct reports figure it out. They know that whatever they bring will be shot down. Who wants to go through that? Who knowingly wants to subject themselves to rejection? And who wants to do it over and over again? My dad would call that type of person a glutton for punishment.

So eventually people stop bringing ideas. They keep them to themselves. They see problems before they appear and opportunities to be gained, but they don't present them. They keep their innovation in the closet where it's nice and safe and the entire team suffers because of it.

The problem is not only that negative leaders miss out on innovation, they impact the people around them with their negativity. What leaders don't realize is that their negativity is contagious. As a friend used to say, "These people are black holes who suck the light out of everyone around them." Or as Sigal Barsade, a Wharton management professor who studies the influence of emotions on the workplace, says, "Emotions travel from person to person like a virus."

Years ago, I was given a team to lead, it was one of my first leadership experiences. My mentor said something I'll never forget. He said, "Tony, you just lost the luxury of having a bad day." I had never thought of it that way. I never considered having a bad day a luxury, but he was right. Having a bad moment is one thing, but allowing it to linger and letting yourself wallow in it is a completely different thing. You may be able to pull that off when you're by yourself, although I wouldn't recommend it. But when you know that you affect a group of people and that your actions and your emotions act as a radio signal looking for someone to tune into your frequency, it's no longer an option. Most people underestimate the control they have over their emotions. It's easy to forget that when there's nothing at stake, but as a leader, your effectiveness and reputation are on the line. Your emotions are a tool. They serve you, you don't serve them.

The bottom line is emotions matter and as a leader, you have a dramatic effect on those around you. A Gallup study by researcher James K. Harter found that business unit sales and profits could be predicted by employees' emotions. People's emotions impact their performance, and if they're healthy and happy, they perform better.

4.   Stay in your lane (delegation)

Delegation is one of those interesting things. We know we should do it and that there are many benefits from it. We know that as a leader, delegating certain tasks allows us to focus our time and energy on the most important things, the ones that have the greatest impact. We know that it can be used as a tool to help properly distribute the workload across our team. We know that when properly used, it is a great method to aid in the development of our team members. We know it reduces our personal workload, it educates and trains our team in vital work skills, and it often will produce better results. People may even be, and often are, enriched and become more committed when given tasks that challenge them or ones they feel will give them needed experience to advance in their career.

That being said, many managers hate to delegate. They avoid it like the plague. They hate it primarily because of two reasons. Everywhere I go, when I ask managers and supervisors why they don't like to delegate, the overwhelming majority of them say the same thing. You know them, I shouldn't even have to say them, but I will.

First, they could do it faster themselves. Second, they want it done right (which means their way.) There are a couple of others that come up occasionally, but in the end, it really all comes down to those two.

Let me be clear: those are two very legitimate concerns. In fact, I would argue that when you first start delegating to an individual, they are both likely true. You can probably do it both better and faster yourself. There are two major problems with doing it yourself instead of delegating.

First, although it you can do the job fast, that also means that you will be doing more work. Part of the reason for delegating in the first place is to offload work so that you're free to do other, more managerial things. If you don't delegate, you have more things to do which likely means that either you won't be able to do them all and something important will not get done, or the quality of your work will suffer because you'll be stretched too thin.

Second, when you don't delegate, you don't develop your team. Delegation allows other associates to do work beyond their normal job function. When you delegate some of your responsibilities to your reports, it helps them to develop the skills necessary to perform at the next level. They get to learn how to do the skills, and you get to assess not only their ability to perform, but also their potential to perform at the next level. Without delegation, you leave a major part of that decision to chance. Without delegation, your direct reports become stagnant.

That stagnation can kill motivation. When people are being developed, and especially when they know it is for the purpose of developing them and possibly helping their career path, they become more ambitious and they take more initiative. When people don't see any potential for growth, they become disengaged.

That being said, there are things you can delegate and things you absolutely should not delegate. The things that you can delegate fall under the category of tasks, projects, and routines. That includes most tasks, especially the ones that are more routine in nature. It also includes projects and duties that require technical expertise. Also included in this should be opportunities to cross-train employees as well as provide challenges and opportunities to break the everyday routine.

The things you should never delegate involve people, problems, and precedents. The responsibility for motivating other employees primarily falls on the leader and shouldn't be delegated. Nor should the evaluation of employees. The resolution of conflict or anything sensitive should not be delegated. And anything that will set a precedent for the future should be handled by the leader.

One of the issues is that most leaders don't really know how to do delegation. They tell their direct reports to do something, but telling isn't delegating. Delegating is more complex and it takes far more skill than just telling people what to do.

It must also be remembered that when delegating, you can't just hand something off to someone else and forget about it. If it was your responsibility in the beginning, you are still the one accountable for its completion. Even though you may delegate that assignment to another, your name is still on it.

When choosing to delegate a responsibility to someone you have to ask yourself, "How much do I you trust that person?" I don't mean do you trust them as a person. There are two specific dimensions of trust that must be considered when dealing with trust. Do you trust their reliability, and do you trust their knowledge, skills, and abilities (KSAs)?

In speaking of reliability, you're assessing whether or not they have the drive and desire to do the task. How ambitious are they? Is there any type of incentive in place or needed? Do they have a history of completing tasks? How reliable are they?

When dealing with KSAs, you're checking to see if the person has the skillset necessary to complete the assignment.

Have they been properly trained in all areas related to the assignment? Do they have knowledge of all the tools necessary to complete the project? Do they have relationships with all the key resources that will be involved in completion of the project?

Once those two questions have been asked, you can refer to diagram 2.

Diagram 2 – Delegation Matrix

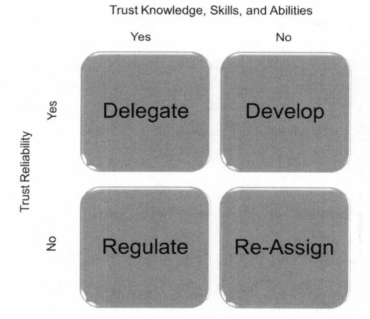

If you have no confidence in either the KSAs or reliability of the person you're thinking about delegating to, you probably need to re-assign that duty to other individuals. You may decide to use this as an opportunity to work with the employee, preparing them for future delegation as well as future opportunities for growth and advancement. If that's the case, I would recommend developing them first. That could easily serve as a means of providing skill creating a greater sense of personal responsibility.

What you don't want to do is delegate an assignment to a person who is neither capable nor motivated to accomplish the assignment. You will endanger your reputation and possibly your career path.

Regulate

If you trust that the person you want to delegate to is capable but does not have a track record of being reliable when assigned tasks, then you regulate them. Regulating is a form of managing in which the delegator sets certain benchmarks in relationship to the completion of the assignment being delegated. Once the benchmarks are set, the delegator then holds accountable the person to complete each benchmark by their due date.

In simple terms, regulating means that when you delegate something to a person who lacks proven reliability, you don't wait until the project is due to find out whether or not they're going to deliver a good result on time. Instead, the delegator gets periodic updates to monitor the progress the person is making on the project. These updates may be periodic based on time (daily, weekly, etc.) or they may be based on certain benchmarks being completed (e.g., task 20%, complete). This allows the delegator to tackle any pitfalls that occur. The delegator can then make determinations as to whether the project will be delayed based on this knowledge. An additional benefit of this strategy is that it can reveal any hidden skill gaps that are present.

Develop

When you have people who are reliable, but you're concerned as to whether they have the skills or ability to complete the assignment, you should develop them. Developing is when the delegator has the person to whom they are delegating follow or shadow them as they are completing the type of task they want to delegate in the future. This is especially important and practical when the task involves a lot of steps or has a lot of details and is going to be done frequently in the future.

The first time the task is to be done, the delegator does the task and has the direct report observe. After the completion of the task, the delegator discusses with the report what they saw, and the delegator offers feedback. Moving forward the direct report takes on more responsibility for the task until the delegator feels confident in the report's ability to complete the task at which point the delegator gives responsibility for the task to the report.

Developing takes a great amount of time. You are not only teaching people how to complete a task, you are bringing them into your world and helping them to see through your eyes. As arduous as this seems, there are two major advantages to doing this.

First, you can be assured the person to whom you are delegating has a complete understanding of what is expected of them. This may seem trivial, but Gallup states that only 50% of employees know what's expected of them. Although I tell managers and supervisors this often, most still underestimate how little or poorly they communicate their expectations to those who will be doing the work. In fact, only 38% of employees report to have managers who help them set expectations. By developing the employee, you will be eliminating one of the most common sources of poor productivity.

Second, developing fixes one of manager's biggest concerns about delegating. Managers not only want things done, they often want things done their way. What better way to make that happen than to have the employee watch you do it and hear your reasoning for why it's being done that way?

If you have full faith in both the ability and reliability of the person you're delegating to, then you are free to delegate the assignment to them. Be careful not to regulate people who have gained your trust in these two areas. That is one of the beginnings of micromanaging. When you micromanage someone, you communicate to them that you don't trust them. As stated previously, delegating is more than simply telling someone what you want done.

Be sure to give your employees all information necessary to complete the job. Be sure your expectations are clear. Be sure they have a clear picture of the assignment. Be sure they understand what all of the deliverables are and how success will be measured, and when they need to be completed. Ask the employee to repeat back to you what you want done in his or her own words to ensure there has been clear communication.

Then, be certain to give the employee the resources and authority needed to carry out the job. Any resources needed should be at the employee's disposal or they should have easy access to them. One of the complaints I most often hear from employees is that they have been given a task with no authority to complete it. Responsibility without authority is a certain recipe for failure.

When the task is completed, evaluate the results, then de-brief the experience with the employee. Remember to address not just what went wrong, but what went right as well. Make sure to give proper recognition for a job well done.

All of this may seem like a lot. It is and it is time consuming, the first time. But as you implement this strategy, over time it will not only be faster, but you will have full confidence that the work being completed meets your standards.

5.   Confront and deal with poor performance

Being in a leadership position means there will be a time when there are performance issues that must be addressed. This is simply part of the job and cannot nor should not be avoided. Before a manager addresses poor performance, there are some issues that should be considered. The leader really needs to either have an idea of the source of poor performance before addressing performance or, instead of addressing the issue, needs to do some questioning and fact-finding. There are three major sources the manager should look for before addressing poor performance.

As stated earlier, the first thing should be to make sure the employee has a clear understanding of what they should do. Although, I do believe the employee has to take some responsibility for knowing their job, in the end the manager is responsible for the employee having a clear understanding of their job responsibilities.

In many cases this should also include the why, not just the what. When employees understand why they're doing a particular task, they either gain greater confidence in the way they have been instructed to complete the task, or they come up with more innovative and possibly more methods for accomplishing the task.

Giving the employee an understanding of why things need to be done also can help the employee prioritize tasks when they've been given multiple items to complete. Unfortunately for most employees, when they receive tasks, they're not told, "I need you to complete this, but no rush, I completely understand that you have other things you're working on." No, instead, it normally goes like this, "Jan, I need you stop what you're doing and do this. It is the most important thing in the world, and if it's not done by the end of the day, life as we know it will cease to exist." Having a knowledge of why things are being done and how they relate to the big picture allows Jan to make educated decisions about her workload.

What should also be considered is the type of feedback the employee has received. Unfortunately, many underperforming employees think they're doing a great job in part because they receive no constructive feedback when their performance isn't satisfactory. Receiving constructive feedback with the intent of helping the employee be a better performer should always be the standard and should always be expected. When this doesn't happen, the employee can gain a false sense of how they really are doing.

This also can happen during performance appraisals. There are times in which the manager, not wanting to hurt the feelings of the employee, tells them that they're doing a great job, when really they are not. Or, because the appraisals are often tied to compensation, the manager doesn't want to punish the employee by giving them a bad review. There are even times when the organization has a culture of giving everyone a high performance score. All of this can contribute to having employees who think they are performing when they aren't. Then they look at you funny when you talk to them about their performance.

Thirdly, are you killing the goose that laid the golden egg? Many of us are familiar with Aesop's fable, *The Goose That Laid the Golden Egg,* or we've at least heard of it. In it, there is a man (or in some versions a man and his wife) who possessed the most amazing goose. Every day the man would collect from the goose's nest a golden egg that he would then sell at the market. Soon the man became rich, but with his wealth came greed.

Over time, the man became greedy. That greed led to impatience. He was upset with the goose because it only laid one egg a day. He couldn't wait for the eggs any longer so one day he came up with the brilliant idea that he would cut the goose open so he could get to all of the eggs at once. When he cut the goose open, he found no eggs, and in the process of looking for more wealth, he had killed his precious goose.

Unfortunately, this happens in the workplace as well. Most leaders have direct reports that produce more than others. They just have the ability and motivation to do more than others. That's the way it is. Most leaders give those top performers more work because they know they can handle it. They have a greater capacity, so it makes sense as a better utilization of resources. The problem is that often there is no reward or benefit to the top performers for doing more work than their coworkers. No bonus, no awards, no "atta boy," nothing.

Years ago, I was doing some work for an engineering firm. One day while I was in the repair area, a new temporary employee was brought in and I got to see his first day. He was given a brief orientation of his assignment, and then he went to work. He was motivated and determined as he knew he had the opportunity to become a permanent employee. About 30 minutes into his shift, I watched as his team leader pulled him aside. He said to the guy, "Slow down." At first, I thought he must be telling him to be more cautious as the equipment he was working on was quite valuable. But the supervisor went on to say, "Look over here. Do you see these four racks? They aren't going anywhere. The faster you fix 'em, the faster they bring 'em in. So, slow down, relax."

I realized at that moment what had happened. This team leader was known to be a high producer. That's why he was the team leader. He quickly realized that the benefits of being a high producer in this organization were minimal. His experience told him that the reward for being a good worker was more work. He actually was being punished for outperforming others, so it only made sense to stop doing the thing that brought punishment.

The presence of any of these sources does not mean the manager can't address the performance. But the manager must realize that when these are present, often the employee is not the problem. The poor performance is the symptom not the disease. The manager will need to address the disease as well as the symptoms.

When you do address the issues, stick to this rule. Praise in public, correct in private. Whenever you address an issue whether performance or behavioral, do it in a private place. Addressing it in public has two adverse effects.

First, you're far more likely to get a bad response or no result when you address it in public. People get defensive when challenged in front of others. Their egos swell and even if they know they're at fault, there's little chance they'll own up to it. Instead they'll either challenge you publicly, which is really bad, or they'll say nothing because they're embarrassed. But you will have not fixed the problem, you will have only made a new enemy.

Second, when you deal with issues in public, you lose credibility. Some people will feel embarrassed for the person you are correcting. Others will take their side. All will feel uneasy. It's a dangerous move to deal with issues in a public way. Praise in public, correct in private.

6. Give employees recognition

Periodically I encounter the executive or business owner who seems almost offended by the thought of giving praise or recognition to his employees. What I normally hear is something like, "Why should I praise someone for something I'm already paying them to do?" I've learned not to spend a lot of time in this situation explaining why or trying to convince them because it is futile.

My normal course of action is to wait until we're in a workshop (if appropriate) and then pose it as hypothetical scenario (so as to not endanger anyone's job). Then I'll pick a person at random and say, "Let's pretend you have a boss who thinks that way. Now I come up and I say, 'Hey, I have an opportunity for you, it pays 10% more than what you're making with an extra week of vacation. Are you interested?'" I've never had anyone say they weren't interested. The question the non-believing boss now must consider is: "How's turnover in their company?"

The problem is that once your mantra becomes "why should I praise them for what I already pay them to do," you've laid the ground rules for how things go. It's all about compensation and that's all. When that's the case, there is no loyalty and you shouldn't expect it. You've told them it's only about money. Loyalty is both earned and reciprocated and money rarely does either. That leaves you and your organization vulnerable. Anyone can easily pick off your best people simply by offering them a little more than you.

If you want to bulletproof your organization from the threat of losing talent to the competition, you need to make sure they receive a consistent dose of recognition. In their book *The Carrot Principle* (Free Press, 2007), Adrian Gostick and Chester Elton state that 79% of employees who quit their jobs cite lack of appreciation as a key reason for leaving (pg. 8).

Praise and recognition are the most powerful tools a leader has in her arsenal to motivate and engage employees. It's also one of the most overlooked tools. Gostick and Elton also report that 65% of North Americans report that they weren't recognized in the least bit the previous year. Yet Gallup[2] links an increase of recognition with lower turnover, higher customer satisfaction, and increased productivity.

Praise and recognition are two of the easiest things a leader can do. It doesn't have to be about money. In fact, unless it's a large amount, it shouldn't be about money. Money gets spent on bills, it doesn't make people feel special. Praising people for a job well done makes people feel special. Honoring them makes them feel special. Awards and certificates, special gifts, even gift cards can make people feel special. Make them feel special and they'll want to do whatever they did to earn the praise again.

7. Accept responsibility for mistakes

We've all had them, the boss that is never willing to admit they were wrong. Even though the mistake is glaringly obvious to everyone, they just aren't willing to either see it, or see it as their fault.

The problem is that everyone else already sees it and knows who was to blame. Whether, it's a function of not wanting to admit to being wrong. Or whether it's feeling too embarrassed to admit it. Whether it's fear of repercussions. Whether it's not wanting to lose the respect of those around you. Whatever the reason, not accepting responsibility for mistakes is an almost universal relationship bank withdrawal.

I often ask people, and you should ask yourself, even though we know that we're supposed to forgive others. Even though we know it benefits not only the person we're forgiving, but it provides liberty for our self as well, is there anyone right now that you are angry with and feel it would be difficult to forgive? Would it make a difference if that person came to you and offered a sincere and remorseful apology? The majority of people say yes. Of course, there are people who've done things to us that were so damaging that an apology just won't do. But for many, that apology, that acknowledgement of fault provides the closure that is needed to move on.

And the irony is that the very things we fear we'll lose if we apologize are the things that are strengthened when we do. We respect people more who take responsibility. People who take responsibility aren't viewed as weaker because of it; they're viewed as strong. Admitting your faults is normally received with compassion, not anger.

But not admitting them when they are obvious can immediately cause others to lose respect. It causes others to view the leaders as weak. The only thing worse than not accepting responsibility is blaming someone else.

The easiest thing to do is just say, "I'm sorry!" Not, "Well mistakes were made." Yeah, but who made them, they didn't just happen? And certainly, not what many politicians have become experts at saying, "I'm sorry if anyone was offended by..." This is a horrible back-handed slap that is essentially saying, "If you weren't so weak I wouldn't have to do this."

Simply saying "I'm sorry!" will not only earn you much greater respect from your team (and your spouse where applicable), but you will be modeling how to take responsibility to your team.

Chapter 14

A MESSAGE TO EXECUTIVES, BUSINESS OWNERS, AND HIRING AUTHORITIES — IT'S NOT ALL THEIR FAULT

Let's be honest, many people are promoted into management for the wrong reasons. Many supervisors become supervisors because they were good at their previous position. If they worked as customer service representatives, they stood out as customer service representatives. If they worked as engineers, they stood out as engineers. If they were sales people, their sales were above average. Most supervisors and managers are promoted first and foremost because of their ability to perform in a non-supervisory position.

But there is a huge problem with this: The skills necessary to succeed in a leadership, supervisory, or managerial role are completely different than those necessary to succeed in a non-managerial role. Many organizations never give this serious consideration when promoting these people into supervisory roles. Instead it is assumed that, because they excelled beyond their peers, they should be rewarded by being promoted above their peers. Yet in reality most don't even have a clue of what to expect in this new role.

Many of these supervisors have received what I like to call *the pitch*. The pitch goes something like this: "Sally, we have been watching you for some time now. Your performance has been exceptional. We've been thinking about your 'career path.' We believe you have a great future with this company. Because of this, we would like for you to take on a new role as a supervisor. We know you'll do a great job, and we look forward to seeing you continue to have tremendous success throughout your career."

That all sounds great, but here is what they don't say: "Now Sally, before you make your decision, you should know that there are three people that you will be supervising who wanted this position and think they deserve it. They *are* going to have a major issue with you and you're going to need to keep them engaged through this transition." They don't say it, but it's often true.

They also don't say, "John, there is a group of prima-donnas that you will need to deal with. They have been **coddled** for some time now, but it's time to get them up to par." They are going to hate the fact that you are calling them to a standard that their previous supervisors wouldn't.

They don't say, "Jennifer, you are really going to need to excel in your people skills because we have two employees with an ongoing feud. They really don't like each other, and I'm concerned that this problem can really escalate into something major."

They rarely if ever say, "And Sally, there is this one employee, he's been a problem for years. Truthfully, this should have been dealt with years ago, but the previous supervisor was a conflict avoider, and let this thing go on for too long. Had the previous supervisor been doing his job, this would have been nipped in the bud a long time ago. But you have now inherited this problem, and you will need to deal with it."

On top of all this, there will be ongoing demands; you will be responsible for the performance of people who feel disenfranchised and underpaid. You will be under-resourced. There will be back stabbing and a competition for resources amongst your new peers. The company works in silos so there will be no sharing of pertinent information between work groups. And, your boss isn't that great of a person either and often won't give you clear direction as to what's expected of you or how to do it, but be certain that she will blame you and throw you under the bus when you don't do it the way she wants."

This is reality, and most new supervisors have no idea it's coming. They're neither emotionally prepared nor have they developed the skills to deal with the onslaught of challenges they're about to face and now there is no turning back. And unfortunately, there is no gracious way to come out of a supervisory role. The character Cypher from the movie "The Matrix" echoes the sentiment of many of these frustrated leaders when he says: "I know what you're thinking, 'cause right now I'm thinking the same thing. Actually, I've been thinking it ever since I got here: Why oh why didn't I take the BLUE pill?"

Regrettably, most companies have no alternative method of rewarding their top performers. It's never even entered their mind. There are many who are very good performers in their field, who in the best interest of everyone involved should remain as such. In fact, for some the best thing their company could do is invest in these individuals so they could develop an even greater proficiency in what they are currently doing. Then they could become subject matter experts and provide even greater value to the organization. But this is rarely done. Too often, the only way to work your way up the ladder and increase your compensation is to take on a supervisory role.

Let's use a football analogy to show how ridiculous this really is. Let's say that on a football team you have eight offensive linemen. Five of the lineman have stood out above the rest so they are named starters, they're the primary one's the team plans to utilize every game. The game depends on these individuals being effective at protecting the quarterback as well as creating holes for the running back to exploit. One lineman, the left tackle, has really stood out as the best lineman on the team. He not only possesses superior athletic ability, his technique is flawless and his ability to pick up blocking schemes and read defenses is unmatched.

So, one day after practice, the coach meets with the tackle to let him know that he'd like him to move to receiver. In his new position, he would have the opportunity to receive more money as well as recognition. He would also directly contribute to the scoring of touchdowns. That would be a horrible idea! The two positions require a completely different skill set. But this happens in the workplace every day. Lineman are moved to receivers, outfielders are moved to catcher, centers are moved to point guards, left wings are moved to goalie, and the team suffers.

And many of these supervisors end up resenting their new roles. They miss being "in the trenches" of whatever they were doing before. They enjoyed the technical aspect of their work and now it's gone. But really, what are they going to do, turn down the opportunity to be more highly compensated for what they bring to the table? Stall their career path because there is no alternative? Until companies figure out how to have an alternative career path that allows people to perform at a high level at whatever they are doing, this problem will continue.

Not only is this not in the best interests of the organization (we need more people who really know their areas expertise inside and out and who love learning more about them), it's not in the best interests of the people they will attempt to lead. Some will be the victims of the supervisor's stress and frustrations as they pass down the pressure they receive to those they lead. Others will never receive enough information to properly do their job, but they will receive negative marks for not hitting a moving target. And the results will be seen in reduced productivity, increased turnover, increased absenteeism, decreased product quality, and reduced customer service.

Fortunately, this is not an insurmountable problem. In fact, the solution is rather simple. Companies must select leaders wisely. Leaders should not be selected by performance alone. In fact, studies consistently show that although current performance is and should be necessary for someone to be considered for a supervisory role, it is not an effective indicator of how a person will perform in a managerial role. Companies must begin evaluating future leaders on a completely different set of KSAs (knowledge, skills, and abilities), KSAs specific to leadership. These should include things like communication skills, interpersonal skills, and problem-solving ability. They need to be coachable, they need to show initiative, and they must be able to handle stress. And did I mention character and integrity? There are other KSAs that great leaders need to possess, but unfortunately many of these you won't be able to see until they are in the position.

On top of all of that, many people are either ill-equipped to handle the pressure and responsibility of leadership or that pressure will expose their weaknesses. They'll become mean. They'll become rude. They'll become selfish. They'll become insecure. Some will think their biting sarcasm is cute and have no idea how much it hurts others.

Some must be weeded out. They are narcissistic, pathological, and couldn't care less about those they manage, they just want to climb the ladder. They were like this before, but it was tolerable. Now they have been empowered and the results could be catastrophic. Their faults will be multiplied throughout their circle of influence. As much as one needs to leverage their strengths to excel, leadership magnifies a people's weaknesses. Let me say that again: **LEADERSHIP MAGNIFIES PEOPLE'S WEAKNESSES.**

Once the right leaders have been chosen, they must be trained. Training can't be limited to what are traditionally called "hard skills": the specific, measurable, teachable, abilities necessary to perform their job function. People must be trained in interpersonal skills. People must be trained in leadership so they can effectively lead others. People must be trained in team building skills so they can take a group of people and transform them into a team. People must be trained to lead people who have different personalities than themselves. They must learn how to resolve conflict (both conflict involving themselves as well as conflict between others). They need to manage their anger as well as any other possible idiosyncrasies they may have. You can't skip this part, it is crucial. In fact, it can't wait until they become managers, it's needed as preparation for the role so they can step into the new position prepared, instead of having to later go back and undo the damage they did when they stepped into the role.

Most organizations do not sufficiently train leaders how to lead other people.

Yet, for most companies, management training is an afterthought at best. The majority of their training resources are focused on hard skills. Employees are often trained how to work the equipment needed to perform their jobs. Salesmen and saleswomen are inundated with training on the entire sales cycle, from prospecting to closing the deal, but when they are promoted, there is rarely a systematic plan to set the new manager up for success. There may well be training on some of the more technical aspects of a person's job, but the idea that managers (especially new managers) will be trained on how to lead, motivate, discipline, and praise the employees assigned them is rare at best. For some unknown reason, these skills are almost completely ignored or taken for granted. And when the economy goes bad, or profits dip, training is the first thing on the chopping block. Not just any training: "nonessential," "non-mission critical training." Soft skill training.

To My Future Force Multipliers

If your company is not providing you training in these areas, go find it on your own. Buy books, go to seminars, and invest in yourself. These skills will provide a great return on the investment you are making. You are the one who's going to benefit the most from it, so don't let anything or anyone keep you from getting what you need. Even if your company isn't providing it, don't let that be an excuse. Go get it on your own! Don't be a casualty of a lack of training.

Become a Force Multiplier!

APPENDIX I – PERSONALITY OVERVIEW

MC

Needs: **Attention,** *Approval, Praise, Popularity*
Leadership Style: Influencer
Strengths:

- life of the party
- loves people
- good talker
- infectious enthusiasm
- creative
- works well in fast moving environments (flexible)
- volunteers for jobs
- thinks up new activities
- appealing personality
- good sense of humor
- emotional and demonstrative
- cheerful
- curious
- inspires others to join

Conductor

Needs: Control, Power, Respect, Recognition
Leadership Style: Driver
Strengths:

- self-motivated
- goal oriented
- ambitious
- very productive and hard working
- very decisive
- moves quickly to action
- makes the goal
- stimulates activity
- dynamic
- not easily discouraged
- independent
- self sufficient
- exudes confidence
- thrives on opposition

Opportunities for Growth:

- talks too much
- doesn't get to the point
- disorganized
- exaggerates (not accurate with numbers)
- no follow through
- speak without thinking
- easily distracted/poor finisher
- very emotional (including in responses)
- doesn't plan or prepare

Opportunities for Growth:

- workaholic
- independent
- must win
- hot-tempered
- controlling (mwohw)
- micromanages at inappropriate times
- intolerant of other's emotions
- demands respect regardless of whether it's been earned

Diplomat

Need: Peace, Trust, Self-Worth
Leadership Style: Stabilizer
Strengths:

- empathetic/sympathetic
- temperate
- great mediator
- good listener
- good at pulling others in

Navigator

Needs: Order, Accuracy, Perfection
Leadership Style: Compliance
Strengths:

- analytical
- organized
- orderly
- detail oriented
- very good troubleshooter

- steady
- peaceful
- low key
- easygoing/relaxed
- patient
- consistent
- quiet but witty
- keeps emotions hidden
- agreeable
- administrative ability

- very high expectations of self and others
- schedule oriented
- thorough
- persistent
- deep and thoughtful
- faithful/devoted
- purposeful
- creative
- self-sacrificing
- economical

Opportunities for Growth

- conflict avoider
- doesn't take risks
- resists change
- too compromising
- self-righteous
- not assertive or goal oriented
- often appears lazy
- can be overly sympathetic
- judgmental

Opportunities for Growth

- focuses on the negatives
- not people oriented
- perfectionist
- slow to make decisions
- easily hurt or discouraged
- unrealistic expectations
- hard to please
- remembering the negatives
- skeptical

As a thank you for purchasing the book, you will receive a discount on the purchase of the Force Multiplier personality assessment. To receive your discount, please use discount code: FO47RC3$BO@K when registering. The assessment can be found at: www.tonychatman.com/forcemultiplier

ENDNOTES

Chapter 3

1. DeAnn Wandler, "The Role of Management in Employee Engagement", *Association for Talent Development*, Monday, October 10, 2016 https://www.td.org/Publications/ Magazines/The-PublicManager/Archives/2016/10/The- Role-of-Management-in-Employee-Engagement

2. Randall Beck and Jim Harter, "Managers Account for 70% of Variance in Employee Engagement," *Gallup Business Journal*, APRIL 21, 2015,

3. Victor Lipman, "Surprising, Disturbing Facts From The Mother Of All Employee Engagement Surveys," *Forbes.com*, 9/23/2013. http://www.forbes.com/sites/victorlipman/ 2013/09/23/surprising-disturbing-facts-from-the-mother-of- all-employee-engagement-surveys/2/

4. Annamarie Mann and Jim Harter, "The Worldwide Employee Engagement Crisis," *Gallup Business Journal*, January 7, 2016. http://www.gallup.com/businessjournal/ 188033/worldwide-employee-engagement-crisis.aspx

5. Amy Adkins, "Majority of U.S. Employees Not Engaged Despite Gains in 2014" *Gallup.com*, January 28, 2015. http://www.gallup.com/poll/181289/majority-employees-not- engaged-despite-gains-2014.aspx

Chapter 13

1. Sonnby-Borgström, M. (2002b). "Automatic mimicry reactions as related to differences in emotional empathy." *Scandinavian Journal of Psychology*, 43, 433–443.
2. John Baldoni, "Employee Engagement Does More than Boost Productivity," Harvard Business Review, July 04, 2013. https://hbr.org/2013/07/employee-engagement-does-more

I wholeheartedly recommend *The Force Multiplier: How to Lead Teams Where Everyone Wins* for its practical insights on team leadership. The book is a straightforward, yet fun read which prepares you to confront the diverse challenges of managing people. Using anecdotes, research, and hard data, Tony Chatman provides real-world solutions to crucial problems facing managers striving to be leaders. Chatman teaches that opposition to change is not a strategy – leaders must incorporate their vision with the team's buy in. This book is a fresh approach to the familiar problems of over managing and under leading; lack of enthusiasm and passion; toxic office politics; interpersonal conflict, and communication problems. We are successfully using Chatman's lessons and putting his advice into everyday practice within our organization.

Captain Steven E. Werse -
International Secretary-Treasurer
International Organization of Masters, Mates & Pilots

The Force Multiplier literally caused me to look in the mirror and ponder the unthinkable—maybe I am the problem! Learning about the weaknesses, strengths, and challenges of not just my personality type but also of others has allowed me to do a better job of communicating and dealing with the wide variety of people I come into contact with on a daily basis. I would recommend this book to everyone—not just management, because we are all managers of our own lives and could benefit from a deeper understanding of our own tendencies in order to become force multipliers for others!

Andrew Mason,
General Counsel, Maine Education Association

Read this book to learn how to get the best out of your team and business. This book will help you to act bigger!

Jeffery Hayzlett,
Primetime TV & Radio Host, Speaker, Author
and Part-Time Cowboy

FINALLY . . . someone is bold enough to address the real issues with managers in the workplace! As a seasoned recruiter for nearly 30 years, I can assure you Tony knows what he is talking about. I love the section that addresses how most people are focused on what to start doing and not on what to **stop** doing. You can receive all the training in the world; however, if those in authoritative positions are not aware of their downfalls, it's all a waste of time. Thank you for addressing this core issue in the workplace, and thank you for such a fresh perspective. I smell a best seller!

Zenja Glass,
President Unlocking Greatness Staffing, Inc.

A book for every leader and leader-to-be to read and share.

There are a LOT of books about leadership, but *The Force Multiplier* is one that gives a humanly practical roadmap of HOW to be a great leader that brings impact to the lives of others. If you're already a leader or want to be one, Chatman's book is one for you to digest and take notes on.

It's full of easy-to-read examples of good (and bad) leadership and gives insight that serves as a mirror to your own style of leadership—for good or for bad.

For every professional who knows they need to improve their leadership abilities, *The Force Multiplier* is a must read.

Ramon Ray, Founder of Smart Hustle Magazine,
Entrepreneur and Global Speaker

This practical leadership book shares strategies you can implement and is full of examples every person can relate to.

I love the idea of being a force multiplier, where the overall effectiveness and output of your group is increased by your presence.

As leaders, we can pay attention to people to create moments that matter to them. Enjoy this book and buy copies for all of your team to create stronger leaders in your organization.

Neen James - Attention Expert - Neen James Inc.

The Force Multiplier may be the most practical leadership book I've read. Tony Chatman is not only an expert in the field of leadership, but he is also an expert at communicating simple truth. This is not your average leadership book, and its impact, specifically on front-line managers, will be extraordinary. As someone who communicates for a living, I highly recommend this work.

Ted Williams III, Host of PBS-WYCC's
The Professors and Chairman of the Social Sciences
Department at Kennedy-King College,
One of the City Colleges of Chicago

I devoured Tony Chatman's *The Force Multiplier*. Taking us from the rare air of the executive suites to the everyday needs of teams and managers, *The Force Multiplier* simply and clearly lays out who you're working with and how to optimize your working relationships. Not only will you better understand your coworkers—whether they're peers, subordinates, or superiors—you'll better understand yourself, as well, ensuring that you won't be "that person" at work and are instead an invaluable asset. If you have a job, you should read this book.

Jeff Christian,
Owner, Muzosa Bujinkan Dojo of NYC